Frank Hopkins

HIDDEN DUBLIN

Deadbeats, Dossers and Decent Skins

MERCIER PRESS
WHAT YOU NEED TO READ

MERCIER PRESS
Douglas Village, Cork
www.mercierpress.ie

Trade enquiries to Columba Mercier Distribution,
55a Spruce Avenue, Stillorgan Industrial Park, Blackrock, County Dublin

© Frank Hopkins, 2007

ISBN: 978 1 85635 568 1

10 9 8 7 6 5 4 3 2 1

 Mercier Press receives financial assistance from
the Arts Council/An Chomhairle Ealaíon

Printed and bound by J.H. Haynes & Co. Ltd, Sparkford.

CONTENTS

For my parents
Frank and Betty Hopkins

ACKNOWLEDGEMENTS

I would like to thank the staff of the National Library of Ireland, National Archives and the Gilbert Library for their help and unfailing courtesy over the years. Thanks are also due to the staff of Mercier Press, particularly Mary Feehan and Eoin Purcell for their insight and encouragement. Special thanks are due to the editor and staff of the *Evening Herald* where the articles first appeared, especially Dave Diebold, Dave Lawlor, Ciarán Burke and Mark Evans.

INTRODUCTION

Dublin has always been full of characters – from the city scavenger Kate Strong to Watty Cox, the wayward publisher. They teem from the pages of history in all their complex glory – the poets, the troubadours, the clowns and conjurers, the mad, the bad and the downright dangerous. The biggest dilemma they created for me – the same hurdle that had to be overcome in the predecessor to this book – was who to leave out.

As in *Rare Old Dublin: Heroes, Hawkers and Hoors*, this book is not intended to be a comprehensive history of Dublin. It offers an eclectic mix of individuals from different walks of life and different periods of time. Like its predecessor it is based on a series of articles written for the *Evening Herald* over the past seven years in the 'Cityscapes' and 'Hidden Dublin' columns.

Although mainly set in eighteenth- and nineteenth-century Dublin there are a number of stories of bizarre antics stretching back as far as the fourteenth century. Some of the characters display enormous capacities for love and life in the most trying of circumstances, others revel in the most heinous of behaviours and others still embark on barmy adventures with often hilarious consequences. All were real people living real lives.

George Barrington, a.k.a. 'Prince of Pickpockets', plied his trade in Dublin in the late eighteenth century before he eventually became chief of police at Parramatta in Sydney while Catholic priest Father Paddy Fay was also transported around the same time for assault, forgery and fraud.

Court cases, hangings, whippings and other punishments are also recurring themes as are tales from the cells and dungeons of the city's prisons. Obviously all of the people mentioned in this category are long dead, so no trouble with the libel laws!

Some characters in the book enjoy varying levels of fame or notoriety and some will be familiar to the casual reader and Dublinologists (try finding that definition for us in the *Oxford English Dictionary*!). The likes of Wolfe Tone, Robert Emmet, Kathleen Clarke, Grace Gifford and the Duke of Wellington are household names in their own right, but the majority of the personalities are not so widely known.

Among the biographical pieces you will find actors, clergymen, scientists, politicians, chancers, conmen, crackpots, eccentrics, rogues and rascals of every hue.

Some of the customs and pastimes of Dubliners were weird, wonderful and often downright strange. Have you ever heard of the 'bearing of balls' – an annual parade by the city's bachelors and the ritual humiliation of would-be bridegrooms at the bullring in the city's corn market. Another candidate in the running for most bizarre ever Dublin custom must be the ancient practice of throwing a horse's head onto the May Day bonfire in the Liberties.

Incidents, accidents, and disasters pepper the history of Dublin. In these pages you will find accounts of shipping disasters such as the sinking of the *Rochdale* and the *Prince of Wales* in November 1807 with the loss of 400 lives. And here too are stories of the calamitous fires that caused so much damage to parts of the city in 1833 and 1875.

The book would not be complete without recounting the whippings, beatings and hangings mostly suffered by the poorest of the poor who populated the tenements of Dublin through the centuries. There's also the occasional tale of derring-do against all odds – for example, the women convicts digging a tunnel out of Newgate prison in 1787.

While I have replicated the style of *Rare Old Dublin: Heroes, Hawkers and Hoors*, this is all new material. I hope it's as pleasurable to read as it was to research and write.

Frank Hopkins
August 2007

Night of the Big Wind

The savage storm on the 'Night of the Big Wind' on 6 January 1839 was one of the worst ever recorded in Ireland and it caused widespread damage. On that night, and for most of the next day, hurricane force winds created havoc throughout the country and in Dublin it was estimated that approximately one house out of every four suffered from some sort of structural damage, ranging from missing roof slates to complete demolition.

On the night of the disaster, several Dublin churches opened their doors to hordes of Dubliners who sought refuge from the storm. Many churches were damaged including St Patrick's Cathedral, St Matthew's at Irishtown and Phibsborough church. The Bethesda Chapel, attached to the Lock Penitentiary and Workhouse in Dorset Street, was burned to the ground. A fire at the chapel had been extinguished on the day preceding the hurricane but the high winds rekindled the fire and by the next morning, chapel, workhouse and six adjoining houses had been reduced to cinders.

Thousands of chimney-stacks throughout the city were demolished by the wind and many of the big houses on St Stephen's Green and Merrion Square suffered structural damage. Many of the city's roads were totally blocked by fallen trees.

Malachi Horan, the Tallaght story-teller, related a tale of how the hurricane destroyed a small silk- and cloth-weaving industry on Killinarden Hill. Malachi, who described the wind as 'God's wrath', said: 'Even the mountain-men near died of the fright that was on them. Like death, the wind come to some, for the others it passed by.' The next morning at daybreak it became apparent that all eight cottages belonging to the weavers had been devastated and they left the area on that very day and never returned.

John O'Donovan, who was working for the ordnance survey in Wicklow at the time, was staying at a hostel in Glendalough. O'Donovan wrote that at the height of the storm, the hostel rocked 'as if it were a ship'. During the night, the wooden shutters of his bedroom were blown in by the storm and he was forced to lie against them until the next morning to keep them closed.

The number of deaths caused by the storm has been impossible to calculate but it has been estimated that between 300 and 400 people lost their lives. At Skerries, nine fishing boats, each with a crew of nine or ten were reported lost. Six people were killed in a fire in Mary Street and in Glasnevin a policeman perished when a wall of the Botanic Gardens fell on him. At Guinness' brewery nine dray horses were killed when a stable wall fell on them.

In the immediate aftermath of the storm, people sought reasons for the calamity that had been visited on them. Some religious folk were convinced that as the storm had taken place on the night of 'Little Christmas' or 'Women's Christmas' it was a sure sign of the wrath of God and that 7 January would be the Day of Judgement. Others simply blamed the fairies for the calamity, while yet another section of the population blamed it on the Freemasons. Apparently, some Catholics were of the opinion that devil-worshipping

Freemasons had summoned his satanic majesty from the nether regions and hadn't been able to send him back again!

Sweep School

Of all the charitable schools ever founded in Dublin surely the 'School for Young Sweeps' must have been the most unusual. This Sunday school was run on the premises of Kellet's School at Drumcondra which had been founded in 1811.

Every Sunday morning, about forty young chimney sweeps assembled at Kellet's where they were given breakfast and kitted out with new shoes, shirts and caps. They were also provided with bars of soap and a few pennies to tide them over during the week.

The occupation of sweep's helper was a dangerous trade to be involved in and the young boys involved were at the mercy of their masters. Warburton, Whitelaw and Walsh's *History of the City of Dublin,* written in 1818, comments on the plight of the sweep's boys: 'no class of the community ... has so much and so deservedly excited public commiseration as that of young sweeps, and we think the existence of such a trade is a reproach to the police of any state where it is permitted ...'

Master sweeps would recruit very young boys, (some as young as seven) as apprentices and send them up the chimney flues to brush and scrape the soot off them. As can be imagined, the occupation of sweeps-boy was a very hazardous one. There were no health or safety regulations to protect these children and among the hazards they faced on a daily basis were the possibility of suffocation from the soot, getting stuck in the chimney, falling from the chimney stacks and even of getting badly burned. There was also a very high incidence of testicular cancer amongst the ranks of the sweep boys which was believed to have been caused by the accumulation of soot.

The school was established following a court case in which a master chimney sweep had been jailed for cruelty to his young apprentice. The master sweep was said to have whipped the boy repeatedly and burned him with coals. The child, who had to be carried into court wrapped in a blanket and covered with ointment, died shortly after the trial. The sweep was sentenced to be publicly whipped and a huge crowd gathered to witness the event.

It was this event that led to the formation of a society for the protection of young chimney sweeps in 1816. At the first meeting chaired by the lord mayor of Dublin tales were recounted of the ill-usage of the apprentices, including several cases of murder. It also emerged that many of the young sweeps were forced by their masters to engage in night-time burglaries. Once the children grew too big to get up the chimneys, they were, apart from the lucky few that went on to become masters themselves, abandoned by the sweep-masters and left to fend for themselves.

The school for sweeps was established with a view to providing those abandoned with a basic education in reading, writing and arithmetic. However, the school was closed after a short period after accusations by Catholic clergymen that the school was a front for the conversion of Catholic children to the Protestant faith.

An act proposing the use of machines to clean chimneys rather than using children was proposed in 1817 but it was never passed. In Dublin it was recommended that a chimney sweeping machine invented by a man called Robinson and endorsed by the Royal Dublin Society be used in order to do away with the necessity of using chimney sweeps altogether. The machine, which used adaptable brushes, was only suitable for square- or rectangular- shaped chimneys and couldn't be used for circular or irregular ones. It was also suggested – quite unrealistically – that Dublin Corporation should force builders to only build chimneys that would be suitable for the machines.

The practice of using children to climb chimneys was finally ended after many years of campaigning in 1864, when the Act for the Regulation of Chimney Sweepers was passed.

Emmet's Grave

Following Robert Emmet's ill-fated rebellion in the summer of 1803 he managed to evade the clutches of the authorities, but was eventually captured on 25 August at Harold's Cross. During his trial for treason at Green Street Court House

Emmet made his famous speech from the dock, which included the often quoted lines: 'Let them and me rest in obscurity and peace; and my tomb remain uninscribed and my memory in oblivion until other times and other men can do justice to my character. When my country takes her place among the nations of the earth, then, and not till then let my epitaph be written.'

While today it can be argued that Ireland has indeed 'taken her place among the nations of the earth' in many aspects of life, it still hasn't been possible to write Emmet's epitaph because we don't know where he is buried.

Emmet was hanged and beheaded outside St Catherine's Church in Thomas Street on 20 September 1803. Following the execution Emmet's remains were taken to Kilmainham Gaol where it is believed that the artist, James Petrie, made a death mask from his severed head.

Emmet's remains were initially buried at Bully's Acre in Kilmainham but were removed soon afterwards and taken to an as yet undiscovered location. Over the years many theories have been put forward as to what happened to Emmet's body but none of these have proved to be conclusive. At least a dozen sites have been examined in searches conducted over the last two centuries, all to no avail.

Currently, the family vault of Dr William Trevor in St Paul's Church in North King Street is being touted as the most likely repository for Emmet's body. Trevor had been governor of Kilmainham Gaol while Emmet had been imprisoned there and it was thought that he was buried there to prevent the grave becoming a shrine and rallying point for Irish republicans.

In 1903 a descendant of Emmet's, Dr Thomas Emmet, who examined a headless skeleton in the vault, claimed that it was that of a twenty-five-year-old man, and said that he was nearly certain it was that of his ancestor. However, tests carried out in 1966 concluded that the skeleton was that of a much older person. The theory now doing the rounds is that the 1903 skeleton was moved elsewhere following Thomas Emmet's examination and substituted with other human remains.

St Mobhi's graveyard in Glasnevin has also been suggested as Emmet's last resting place. George Petrie, son of James Petrie who made Emmet's death-mask, claimed in a letter that Emmet had been buried there at the dead of night.

There have been numerous other suggestions in relation to possible locations of Emmet's grave, including St Michan's in Church Street, St Peter's in Aungier Street (now covered by the YWCA building) and even St Catherine's Church where Emmet was executed.

Other theories suggest that Emmet's remains now lie in a disused Protestant graveyard at Blennerville in County Kerry and it has also been claimed in the past that his body was buried in the grounds of John Philpot Curran's house, The Priory in Rathfarnham.

Even spiritualists have been enlisted on occasion to help with the search. In 1978 a Californian medium claimed to have 'divined' the presence of Emmet's skull in a vault beneath St Catherine's whilst under the influence of hypnosis. The vault which belonged to the earl of Meath was opened and a skull was discovered but it was thought to have belonged to a member of the earl's family. Another medium later claimed that he had visualised Emmet's skull under a house in Ringsend.

Napper Tandy

The name of James Napper Tandy, United Irishman and colourful Dublin character, has largely been forgotten. Today most people are familiar with Tandy's name courtesy of the song 'Wearing of the Green' while his house is mentioned in the old Dublin ballad 'The Spanish Lady'.

James Napper Tandy was born in the Cornmarket area of Dublin in 1740. His father John was an ironmonger and a serving member of the Holy Trinity Guild of Merchants. Very little is known about Tandy's early life in the Cornmarket but in 1962, Dublin Corporation removed a plaque commemorating Tandy from 7 High Street before demolishing the building.

Tandy worked in the family business of ironmongery for a time but later went into business as a land agent and rent collector. In 1760 he was admitted as a freeman to the Merchants' Guild and in October 1788 he was elected junior master of the guild.

He was also senior master of one of Dublin's oldest guilds, the Guild of St Anne, which had connections with St Audoen's Church beside Christchurch.

Tandy was elected to the City Assembly in 1777 as a representative of the Merchant's Guild and he served the city in this capacity for nearly eighteen years. He was active in many issues at that time including a campaign against the relocation of the Custom House from Wellington Quay to its present location. Tandy and the merchants of the city were against the proposed move on the basis that it would lead to greater expense and inconvenience to them.

Tandy himself led a riot in opposition to the Custom House in 1781 and the architect James Gandon, described what happened when Tandy 'followed by a numerous rabble, with adzes, saws, shovels etc. came in a body on the grounds and levelled that portion of the fence which had been thrown up adjoining the North Wall and River Liffey'.

Tandy enlisted in the duke of Leinster's regiment of the Dublin Volunteers in 1778 and he was given command of the artillery section. He was later given command of the Irish brigade of the Dublin Independent Volunteers. Later on, Tandy became secretary of the Dublin branch of the United Irishmen whose membership included Wolfe Tone, Thomas Russell and Oliver Bond.

The United Irishmen were proscribed in 1792. Tandy was forced to flee to America during the following year after falling foul of the police and he continued to work for the United Irishmen there. Tandy's movements in America were eagerly followed by the newspapers back in Ireland. A report in the *Freeman's Journal* in November 1793 claimed that he had been seen in Philadelphia: 'The presence of this poor gentleman seems extremely ominous to civic communities.' Two months later the same newspaper reported: 'The last accounts from citizen Tandy place him in Boston. Heaven forfend that good city from plague, pestilence and sedition.'

Tandy came into contact with a French diplomat named Pierre Adet in America who described him as 'an excellent republican, a man entirely devoted to France and hating England as much as he is attached to our cause'.

Tandy went to Paris in 1797 where he managed to persuade the French to take part in an invasion of Ireland. The French made him a general and in September 1798 he landed in a French brig the *Anacreon* at Inis Mhic a Duirn (Rutland Island) off the coast of Donegal.

On landing, Tandy raised an Irish flag and issued a proclamation that was optimistically dated 'The first year of Irish Liberty'. On learning of General Humbert's defeat Tandy withdrew and sailed for Norway. He eventually made his way to Hamburg where he was captured and extradited to face trial for treason in Ireland.

He was sentenced to death after his trial at Lifford in Donegal but was released following the intervention of Napoleon Bonaparte. He returned to France where he was awarded a full general's pension and he died at Bordeaux on 24 August 1803.

James' Street

Today the fame of James' Street in Dublin is recognised worldwide on account of its association with Ireland's best-known export for the last 240 years – Guinness. However, in terms of history, the street has much more to offer than tales of Uncle Arthur's 'black protestant porter'.

There were at least fifty small breweries in the district 200 years ago, not to mention the twenty-five distilleries. At that time there were seven other breweries in James' Street besides Guinness' along with a half dozen distilleries. The Poddle River was still largely above ground and it was considered to be ideal for the manufacture of beer. One hundred years later many of these breweries had gone to the wall and only three – including Guinness' – were left in James' Street. The other two surviving breweries, Manders & Powell and the Phoenix Brewery joined forces in 1890 but had gone bust by the time the First World War started.

A local legend concerning the Manders Brewery and Robert Emmet is recounted in a history of the area written by Martin Fitzpatrick in 1994 to celebrate the one-hundred -and-fiftieth anniversary of St James' parish. Apparently many locals believed that the Manders Brewery 'went into long and painful decline' because some of the company's barrels had been used as part of the scaffolding used in Emmet's execution on Thomas Street in 1803.

The Phoenix Brewery was originally owned by a man called Madder and he subsequently sold it to Daniel O'Connell junior, a son of 'The Liberator'. Guinness eventually took over the premises of the two breweries following their closure in 1914.

Another place of interest in James' Street is the graveyard at the back of the Protestant church. The graveyard, which catered for all religions, was at one time one of the largest in the city and it appears to have been in use from as early as the thirteenth century. The earliest reference to a burial there was in 1495.

It has been speculated that an earlier church, dedicated to St James of Compostella, patron saint of lepers, was situated in or around this site. It's not clear when this church was built but the first reference to it was in the mid-thirteenth century.

Close to the cemetery is an ornamental fountain believed to have been built on the site of the well in 1790. Many writers have spoken about a curious tradition of carrying a corpse three times around this fountain on their way to be interred at St James' graveyard. This practice was carried on up until the 1940s and is believed to have evolved during the Reformation period to allow time for the recital of prayers for the dead. Catholic priests were banned from performing these ceremonies in Protestant graveyards at that time. The graveyard was officially closed during the 1950s to all but those with burial rights.

During medieval times, on 25 July, the feast day of St James was celebrated by a fair held just outside the graveyard. Although it didn't rival the great fair at Donnybrook, St James' Fair usually ran for about a week and attracted traders and merchants from all over Europe.

The fair was usually accompanied by excessive drinking and carousing that sometimes led to rioting and even death. The fair was eventually banned in the 1730s, but a scaled-down version of it continued to be held outside the graveyard for many years afterwards.

Four Courts

The copper-topped dome of the Four Courts on the north side of the Liffey is one of the most instantly recognisable images of Dublin City, but it is not widely known that for hundreds of years the courts were held on the south bank of the river.

The first Inn of Court was established outside the city walls on the site where Exchequer Street now stands during the reign of Edward I. Because the court was outside the walls of the city it was harder to defend and the Wicklow men attacked it and burnt it to the ground. Afterwards the four courts of the chancery, king's bench, exchequer and common pleas were held for a period at Dublin Castle and at Carlow.

In 1606 the Inn of Court moved across the river to its present location for a short time but due to pressure from Dublin Corporation, which wanted to keep them within the confines of the old city, the courts moved back across the Liffey in 1608 to a new home at Christchurch. By the end of the seventeenth century the courts were in a very dilapidated condition and the architect William Robinson was commissioned to rebuild them. Despite Robinson's efforts, by 1755 the Four Courts were in ruins again and a decision was taken to build a new structure across the Liffey.

In order to gain entry to the old Four Courts, visitors had literally to go through 'Hell'. Christchurch was at one time surrounded by a warren of narrow lanes and alleyways. One of these passages to the west of the cathedral known as 'Hell' is said to have taken its name from an underground cellar known by the same name. A large wooden statue of the devil adorned the arched entrance to the alley. An unnamed traveller quoted in John Gilbert's *History of the City of Dublin* said of the effigy: ' … over the arched entrance there was pointed out to me the very image of the Devil, carved in oak, and not unlike one of those hideous black figures that are still in Thomas Street, hung over tobacconists' doors.'

The old courts continued in use up until 1796 and one of the strangest trials ever witnessed took place there in 1795. In April of that year the Reverend William Jackson was tried and convicted of planning a French invasion of Ireland. Rather than wait for the judge, Lord Clonmel (better know to Dubliners as copper-faced Jack), to pass the death sentence on him, Jackson took poison and died standing in the dock before Clonmel could pass judgement on him. His body was left in the dock overnight and an inquest held the following day revealed that he had taken 'a large quantity of metallic poison'. It later emerged that he had mixed arsenic and aquafortis with his tea.

Jackson was buried in St Michan's churchyard and Jonah Barrington in his *Personal Sketches* says that despite having committed treason and suicide, Jackson had a 'splendid funeral' that was attended by several members of parliament.

Work on the present Four Courts didn't commence until 1776 when Thomas Cooley began work on the Public Records Office. When Cooley died in 1784 James Gandon took over the project and the building was largely complete by 1802.

Oliver Bond

The name's Bond, not James but Oliver Bond, another 'forgotten man' of Dublin's history who is now chiefly remembered by the street named after him as well as Oliver Bond House, the Dublin Corporation flat complex built in the 1930s.

Originally from Derry, Bond had a prosperous woollen drapery business in Pill Lane in 1783 and two years later he had moved to a larger building at 13 Bridge Street. Bond joined the United Irishmen in 1791 along with his friend Simon Butler. He was soon fined £500 and served his first stint in Newgate Prison, having been found guilty of sedition.

The six-month prison term didn't impose too much strain on Bond and Butler as they were allowed the run of the prison and they could consume as much food and drink as they could get in from the outside. This must have been a fairly substantial amount as they managed to run up a wine bill of £500 during the period of their incarceration.

On 12 March 1798, fifteen members of the Leinster Directory of the United Irishmen, including Bond, were arrested during a meeting at his house in Bridge Street. They had been betrayed by another United man Thomas Reynolds, who had been sworn into the society by Lord Edward Fitzgerald.

The men were charged with high treason and taken to Newgate Prison. Bond's trial took place in July of 1798 and he was found guilty and sentenced to death.

The judge ordered that Bond be taken to the gallows and 'hanged by the neck, but not until you are dead, for while you are yet living, your bowels are to be taken out and thrown in your face, and your head is to be cut off, and your head and limbs to be at the King's disposal, and may the Lord have mercy on your soul'.

However, twenty minutes before the execution was due to take place, Bond received news from the sheriff that he was to be reprieved. On the morning of 6 September 1798, Bond was found dead in his cell at Newgate in very mysterious circumstances. The next morning, the official explanation for his death was that he had died from apoplexy but few, if any, believed that this was the real reason.

The evening before, Bond had been in perfect health and was seen playing hand-ball in the prison yard and it was generally believed at the time that he had been murdered by one of the jailers for a reason that has never been established.

Some reports make the claim that a turnkey called Gregg was responsible for Bond's death, while the finger of suspicion was also pointed at another jailer called Simpson. A letter written by Bond's neighbour James Davock recounted in R.R. Madden's *Lives of the United Irishmen* claimed that Bond had been strangled by Simpson during a riot in the prison.

Yet another claim published in a newspaper many years after said that Bond had died after one of the warders had struck him on the back of the head with a heavy kettle. Bond was buried in St Michan's in a grave belonging to his wife's family.

If Oliver Bond is one of the forgotten men of Dublin's history, then surely his wife Eleanor, a daughter of the Church Street iron founder, Henry Jackson, is the forgotten woman. She played an active role in all the activities of the United Irishmen and she kept the woollen business going while her husband was in prison.

Eleanor played an active role in the recruitment and swearing in of other women to the society. She was also concerned with the welfare of the political prisoners in Kilmainham and at Christmas in 1796 she sent the prisoners a pie that contained newspapers, correspondence and writing materials.

Following her husband's death, Eleanor continued to run the family business until 1809 when she emigrated to Baltimore with her four children. She died there in 1843.

McCready

The standard work on the origins of our city street names was first printed over 100 years ago and is still the most authoritative reference book. *Dublin Street Names Dated and Explained* by the Reverend C.T. McCready was first published by Hodges Figgis & Co in 1892. The first edition was limited to a print run of 500 copies, some of which were to be had for half-a-crown while the hardback version sold for three shillings each.

McCready, a Dubliner himself, was educated at Trinity College and ordained in 1866. He worked as curate in several south inner city parishes, including St Audoen's and St Ann's, and he later became a minor canon at St Patrick's Cathedral.

McCready's book contains a wide range of interesting information on the origins of the names of the highways and byways, lanes and alleyways of Dublin. The book was organised under different headings such as: the bridges of Dublin, gates of Dublin, quays of Dublin, streets named after saints and the statues of Dublin. McCready also provides what he called a 'rough classification' of the sources of the names of Dublin's streets, most of which fall under the categories of churches, kings and queens, lords lieutenant, lord mayors, noblemen and owners of property.

However, most of the interesting Dublin street names are those listed under the categories of occupation, corruptions and physical characteristics.

One name which could be described as occupational was Love Lane, which was changed in 1733 to Little Cuffe Street and in 1776 to French Street. McCready says that the change occurred 'on account of previous bad repute'. The area had been one of the main red-light districts in the city.

Another occupational name that speaks for itself was Washerwoman's Lane in St Catherine's parish. Interestingly, six out of the twelve names listed in this section were mentioned as far back as the twelfth century, the earliest being Sutor Street or the Street of the Shoemakers, first mentioned in 1190. The other five are Cook Street, Potter's Street, Saddler's Street, Skinner's Row and the Street of the Taverners (Winetavern Street).

Several Dublin streets got their names from their physical characteristics; Dirty Lane, now Bridgefoot Street, obviously didn't get its name because you could eat your dinner off the ground there. The names of Hill Street and High Street need no further explanation. Hind Street (formerly known as the street of the shoemakers) was another name for Behind Street, so called because it was behind Skinner's Row.

One very curious name mentioned in the book that we all take for granted today is Dolphin's Barn. McCready gives no information on the origin of this name but other sources say that it was once known as Dunphy's Barn. He also mentions a place called Dolphin's Lane (now Golden Lane) and he speculates that the name could have arisen from a tavern there with a sign of the Dolphin hung outside.

McCready also lists several taverns that have given their names to some laneways and yards in the city. Blue Boar Alley at the southern end of Werburgh Street was one of these. Boot Lane, now a part of Arran Street, took its name from a place called the Boot Inn, while an establishment called the Blue Hand in Pill Lane gave its name to a lane, a yard and a court.

The Muglins

Just to the north of Dalkey Island in Dublin Bay, there are three tiny rocky outcrops called Lamb Island, Clare Rock and Maiden Rock. Close by is another group of rocks known as the Muglins. In 1766, the bodies of two pirates were hung in chains there as a warning to other would-be transgressors of the law.

In November 1765, a Scottish seaman Captain George Glas, in partnership with a Captain Cochrane, were on their way from the Canary Islands to London aboard *The Earl of Sandwich*. The ship was laden with a cargo of silk, gold dust, jewels and a large quantity of Spanish dollars. In mid-journey, four of the crew, George Gidley, Andreas Zekerman, Richard St Quintin and Peter McKinlea, an Irishman, took over the ship. Captain Cochrane was beaten to death with an iron bar while Captain Glas was stabbed to death and thrown overboard. Glas' wife and daughter also perished when they were thrown over the side by McKinlea. The four then set sail for Ireland and as they approached the coast near New Ross they scuttled the ship, killing the last remaining crew in the process, and made off in a longboat stuffed with as much booty as it would hold.

They landed near Duncannon Fort on 3 December 1765 and buried most of their loot on the beach in a small bay which, since the incident, has been known as Dollar Bay. Stuffing their pockets with as many Spanish dollars as they could carry, the men set off for the village of Fishertown near New Ross. The four spent a few hours there and managed to get so drunk that they were robbed of $1,200.

The next day they travelled to New Ross where they laundered some of their cash and bought pistols and horses. However, they spent so much money in New Ross that they managed to attract the attention of the authorities who suspected the four of piracy. Suspicion deepened further when the wreck of *The Earl of Sandwich* was blown ashore soon afterwards.

Meanwhile, the four pirates decided that it would be prudent to get out of New Ross so they travelled to Dublin, where they took rooms at the Black Bull Tavern in Thomas Street.

The sheriff of Ross sent an order to the mayor of Dublin to arrest the men and St Quintin and Zekerman were captured and brought to Newgate Gaol. Gidley and McKinlea were arrested later in a coach bound for Cork. When questioned, the four admitted their guilt and revealed the whereabouts of the buried treasure to the authorities.

The four pirates were tried for robbery and murder on 1 March 1766. They were found guilty of the crimes and all four were sentenced to death. Two days later they were taken by military escort to St Stephen's Green where they were hanged on the gallows. The bodies were taken back to Newgate Prison and from there they were taken in the black cart (an early version of the meat wagon) to be hung in chains at the Great South Wall below Ringsend. Two of the bodies were put on display at Mackarell's Wharf and the other two were hung up at the Pigeon House itself.

Initially, the bodies of the pirates provided a macabre sideshow for strolling Dubliners but after a few week's interaction with the Ringsend seagulls the attraction began to fade somewhat. Walkers began to complain about the offensive sight and smell of the corpses and on 1 April the newspapers announced that the bodies of McKinlea and Gidley were to be removed to the Muglins near Dalkey Island. A gallows was erected on the Muglins and the two bodies were hung up in a new set of irons 'said to be the completest ever made in the kingdom'.

Dame Street

The name of Dame Street which stretches from Cork Hill to College Green has its origins in the eastern gate of the old city walls of Dublin.

In medieval times, even before the Anglo-Norman invasion of Ireland, the eastern gate of the walled city of Dublin was known as 'La porte de Sainte Marie del dam' and had a statue of the Virgin Mary placed above it. This gate, also known as Dam's or Dame's Gate, and the thoroughfare leading to it, were extremely narrow and as the prosperity of the town grew, it became necessary to widen the thoroughfare and the gate by knocking down a portion of the city wall in 1698. Earlier attempts had been made to remove the gate but some residents who had houses adjoining the wall had objected to the proposed demolition.

This gate was the site of a major confrontation between the occupying Normans and the Vikings, who under the leadership of Asculv Mac Thorkil made an attempt to regain the city in 1171. 'John the Mad' an ally of Mac Thorkil's attacked the gate which was defended by the Norman Miles de Cogan. Giraldus Cambrensis, in his *Expugnatio Hibernica*, which was written during the 1180s, described the attack on the gate: 'They were warlike figures, clad in mail in every part of their body after the Danish manner. Some wore long coats of mail, others iron plates skilfully knitted together, and they had round, red shields protected by iron round the edge. These men, whose iron will matched their armour, drew up their ranks and made an attack on the eastern gate.'

The 'riding of the franchises' of the city always commenced by riding out through this gate and a description of the procession written in 1488 says: 'They proceeded well horsed, armed and in good array, taking their way out of Dame's-gate, turning on their left hand to the Strand ...'

At the eastern end of Dame Street, the boundary with College Green (then Hoggen Green) was marked by Hogges Gate which later came to be known as the Blind-Gate. This was removed in the early 1660s as it was in imminent danger of collapse.

At that time the banks of the Liffey were not walled in and there was a small harbour in close proximity to the gate. In 1534, the archbishop of Dublin, John Allen, boarded a boat at this harbour in an attempt to escape the clutches of 'Silken Thomas' Fitzgerald. However his boat was blown back onto the shore at Clontarf and he was murdered at Artane Castle.

Throughout the eighteenth and nineteenth centuries, Dame Street was home to a thriving newspaper and book publishing trade. Not surprisingly Dame Street was also well supplied with taverns and 'groggeries' such as the Half Moon Ale House, the Robin Hood and the Still, which was famous for its whiskey. However, all of these establishments paled in comparison with Patrick Daly's chocolate house which stood at 2 and 3 Dame Street. Daly's was one of the best-known clubs in Ireland at the time and it was mainly frequented by members of the upper classes. It was particularly noted as a gambling joint and it was said that half the landed estates in Ireland had changed hands there during its time. The club was also one of the watering holes favoured by the bucks and rakes of the city and it wouldn't have been unusual to see some of the patrons being thrown through the windows. Duelling with pistol and sword was a commonplace occurrence at the club and there were even tales of club members using the statue of St Andrew in St Andrew's Church for target practice!

Provost Prison

The last letters ever written by Theobald Wolfe Tone in November 1798 contained the address 'Provost Prison, Dublin Barracks'. Dublin Barracks, or the Royal Barracks, is now Collins Barracks and the old Provost Prison has long since been demolished.

Tone was taken prisoner at Lough Swilly, County Donegal, on 12 October 1798 and upon his arrival in Dublin he was taken to the Royal Barracks where he was incarcerated in the Provost's Prison which was, at that time, under the supervision of the infamous Major Sandys. Sandys combined with the Dublin Town majors, Swan and Sirr, to create an unholy trinity which conducted a reign of terror on the citizens of Dublin during and after the 1798 rebellion.

On the day of his trial, Tone was brought from the Provost's Prison dressed in a French officer's uniform consisting of 'a large cocked hat, with broad gold lace and the tricoloured cockade; a blue uniform coat, with gold embroidered collar, and two large gold epaulets, blue pantaloons, with gold-laced garters at the knees; and short boots bound at the tops with gold lace'. After Tone was sentenced to be executed in front of the 'new prison' he was taken back to his cell where he was discovered on the following Monday with his throat cut.

The old Provost Prison, originally built as a coal yard and then used as a bake-house, was sited at Drury Lane in the barracks, just off Palatine Square, and it was described as containing two 'black holes' that could accommodate approximately five prisoners each, and two large cells that were said to be twenty feet wide and twenty-eight feet long. These cells usually held anything up to twenty prisoners each, but more could be accommodated in times of crisis such as in 1798.

In June 1800 a daring escape was undertaken from the Provost Prison by forty-six prisoners who were suspected of having links with the United Irishmen. The prisoners escaped by digging a tunnel from one of the 'black holes' in the Provost, under the perimeter wall of the barracks and out onto Arbour Hill. Some of the prisoners were foiled by the deputy provost marshal, William Blair, who had been out buying meat for the prison at the time. Giving evidence to a court of inquiry set up to investigate the escape he recounted seeing prisoners emerging from a hole close to the barrack master's stores and fleeing into the fields at the back of Arbour Hill. Blair managed to prevent the other prisoners from escaping by throwing iron pots of meat down into the hole and blocking it up.

Faulkner's Dublin Journal of 28 June 1800 gave some details of the escape. The report described the escapees as 'fifty criminals' who had gotten out of the prison 'by undermining the wall and excavating a passage through the high bank of earth between the Barracks and Arbour Hill. Amongst those who escaped were the notorious villains and murderers Hughes and Shaughnessy ...' *Faulkner's Journal* also reported that Hughes and Shaughnessy, who were 'under sentence of death', had escaped from prison twice before. No details of their crimes were given.

Another newspaper report of 1 July reveals that three of the prisoners were recaptured in the Dublin Mountains by five soldiers of the Lower Talbotstown Cavalry.

The Court of Inquiry recommended the closure of the old Provost Prison, and a new prison on the site of St Bricin's Military Hospital was in place by 1803.

James Clarence Mangan

Many years ago, Lord Edward Street, opposite Christ Church, formed the upper part of Fishamble Street and number three, now occupied by the Castle Inn, was the birthplace of the poet James Clarence Mangan.

Mangan, born on 1 May 1803, one of four children, was the son of a poor shopkeeper. He later blamed his parents for all of his shortcomings. In his autobiography he mentions 'the honour or the disreputability of having been born the son of a grocer'. His father had originally been a schoolteacher from Shanagolden in Limerick and in 1801 he married Catherine Smith, owner of a small grocery shop in Fishamble Street. Throughout his life Mangan often referred to his father's bullying ways and he once said that he had treated him and his siblings 'as a huntsman would refractory hounds'.

Mangan received his first schooling from a Jesuit priest, Father Austin, at a school in the nearby Saul's Court where he is said to have studied the basics of Latin, French, Spanish and Italian. Mangan was forced to transfer to another school in Darby Square at the age of eleven when his father's business went bust; and in 1818, when he was declared bankrupt for the eighth time, the younger Mangan was forced to become the family breadwinner.

At the age of fifteen Mangan began work as an apprentice in a scrivener's office in York Street. The work of a scrivener involved the tedious task of copying legal documents by hand and Mangan laboured long and hard at this profession for nearly seven years.

Mangan took up writing as a pastime during his time in the scrivener's office and he contributed poetry, puzzles and other items to a variety of publications. During the 1830s he wrote for *The Comet*, a weekly satirical newspaper. Some of his writings were so strange at that time that one of his contemporaries concluded that he had to be an opium-addict, even at that young age. He was also a regular contributor to the *Dublin University Magazine*.

In 1838 Mangan was recommended for a position in the Ordnance Survey office by Dr George Petrie. He stayed there until 1842 when he began work as a clerk in the library at Trinity College and he supplemented his small income with contributions to the *Nation* and the *Irish Penny*

Journal. By that time Mangan was drinking very heavily and his favourite haunts were The Bleeding Horse in Camden Street, The Star and Garter and The Phoenix Tavern in D'Olier Street. He was also fond of smoking opium but it's not clear if he was actually addicted to the stuff. Mangan turned his hand to translations of Irish poetry and *Dark Rosaleen*, Mangan's finest work, was published at that time

Ireland was devastated by a cholera epidemic in 1849. Mangan contracted the deadly disease in May of that year and he was brought to a temporary hospital set up in Kilmainham known as the 'cholera sheds'. Mangan left after a few days and made his way to what would be his last home – a run-down garret in Bride Street.

Mangan was taken to the Meath Hospital on 13 June and he died there a week later. The poet knew that he was dying and he spent his last days in the Meath scribbling notes on any scrap of paper that he could find. Alas, Mangan's last writings were burned by an attendant immediately after his death as she had been reprimanded earlier for not keeping the wards tidy.

Cholera victims were supposed to be buried immediately after death but Mangan's funeral didn't take place until three days later. The cholera epidemic of 1849 had killed thousands and there weren't enough coffins or hearses to go round. Mangan's remains were interred at Glasnevin cemetery on 23 June 1849 and the funeral was attended by only five of his closest friends.

An obituary penned by his friend Joseph Brennan appeared in the *Irishman* on the day of his funeral. It said of him: 'His genius was a Midas-gift, which came saddled with a curse ... It is enough to say that he was the greatest of our modern poets; that he was unrivalled as a translator ... that a truer bard, in nature, as in genius, never lived than our poor friend Mangan ...'

Hibernian Marine School

On 28 June 1766, the *Freeman's Journal* announced that: 'the Governors of the new charitable institution of an Hibernian Nursery for the Marine have taken a house at Ringsend, which is now fitting up, where they propose to lodge, diet, clothe and instruct 20 Boys, the Orphans or Children only of decayed Masters of Ships, or of Mariners, unable to support their families, who are to be received from the Age of seven to ten years and apprenticed at thirteen or fourteen or sooner (according to the fitness and constitution of the Boys) to Masters of Ships.'

Earlier that year, a group of Dublin merchants, ship owners and others had banded together to provide a boarding school in Ringsend for the education of young boys whose fathers had been lost at sea and for the sons of sailors who were unable to afford to educate them.

The scheme was initially funded by private donations and a levy of three pence per month on the wages of Dublin sailors. By the end of September 1766 the school, called the Hibernian Marine School, was providing food, shelter and instruction in seamanship, navigation, gunnery, tailoring and shoe-making for seventeen young boys, the majority being orphans. A year later there were forty boys in the institution.

In 1769 the governors decided that the house at Irishtown was too small for its purposes and they managed to lease a plot of land at John Rogerson's Quay from the developer Luke Gardiner for an annual rent of £70. The board then petitioned the government for funds to build a new school between Cardiff's Lane and Lime Street at John Rogerson's Quay that would be capable of accommodating 200 children.

The new and improved school, designed by either Thomas Cooley or Thomas Ivory, was described in a Government report of 1809 as a 'plain substantial building, seventy-two feet by forty-six, with two wings, each thirty feet in front by sixty feet in depth ...'

There were rooms for the master, chaplain, usher and house-keeper, an infirmary, laundry, mess-room and dormitories at the school. The boys were entitled to three meals each day and a typical day's rations consisted of burgoo (watery porridge) and bread for breakfast; dinner was usually a bowl of ox-head soup with peas and bread, and for supper each boy received three ounces of bread and a mug of milk. Sunday dinner was the highlight of the week with boiled beef, potatoes, vegetables and beer being served.

Rules were strictly enforced and any breaches of discipline were punishable with expulsion. Minor crimes and misdemeanours were punished with a liberal dose of the cat-o'-three-tails (presumably a junior version of the cat-o'-nine-tails).

In 1809 the school's governors and staff were criticised

for the inefficient running of the school and there was a rise in the numbers of children absconding from it. Since 1800 an average of twelve boys per annum had absconded, but in 1807 and 1808, forty boys had gone missing. There were also complaints from ships' captains about the poor quality of instruction in navigation and general education given to the boys and both the master and usher were fired during that year.

By the mid 1850s there were less than thirty boys in the school and it was destroyed by fire in 1872. The Marine School moved to a new house at Upper Merrion Street in 1900. It was again relocated to a house in Rathmines. In 1904 the school found a more permanent home across the bay at Seafield Road in Clontarf where it was in use until 1968 under the name of the Mountjoy Marine School.

The Marine School eventually amalgamated with the Bertrand Russell School and subsequently formed Mount Temple Comprehensive School in 1970.

Dublin Oil

The 14 February edition of the *Evening Herald* in 1903 contained a story concerning an oil well discovered in the cellar of a house in the north inner city of Dublin near Mountjoy Square.

The oil well had been discovered five weeks earlier in the basement of a dwelling house at 100 Summerhill and was causing ripples of excitement among the ranks of the British oil industry. The house had been built on ground reclaimed from bogland. One hundred years ago many 'experts' believed that oil was to be readily found in Irish bogs.

When the oil was first discovered, it was said to have flowed in abundance for three days and then slowed down for two weeks and then flowed strongly ever since.

A geologist, Professor Grenville Cole, sent a sample of the oil to London for analysis and was eagerly awaiting the results. Cole believed that the liquid bubbling in the basement at Summerhill was crude petroleum and that the amount of oil already produced from the well would justify it being worked as a commercial venture. Cole was confident that further investigation of the basement would yield positive results.

Another report in the *Evening Herald* a week later, on 20 February, was just as optimistic but added a noted of caution: 'That it is a genuine strike appears beyond doubt, but whether the yield will justify all the expense of boring and development remains to be seen.'

The editor of the *Petroleum* magazine described the oil as a white substance that smelled strongly of paraffin. The magazine was said to have great faith in the find. When asked if he thought that the Summerhill find was significant he predicted that large quantities of the oil would be found, 'such as will surprise the good people of Dublin who probably have no idea of the immense profits made out of a fairly good oil-well'. However, the story of the Summerhill oil well was quickly forgotten about when the oil was found to have little or no commercial value.

Another oil story appeared in a newspaper report of 24 February under the bizarre heading of 'The Evil One In Ireland's Eye'. Apparently the Summerhill oil-well story had strengthened the belief in British circles that oil was to be found in great quantities in Ireland. The newspaper reported that the British government was about to look for oil in several different parts of the country and geologists were very hopeful of success.

Ireland's Eye was one of these places mentioned. One night, ten years earlier during a severe storm, blue flames were seen shooting up from the island and some Howth locals on the mainland attributed the phenomenon to the presence of the devil on the island.

However, a geologist who visited the island to find out what had caused the flames had a different explanation. Earlier that year a group of day-trippers had lit a fire on the island to boil a kettle and reported afterwards that the fire had eaten its way well into the ground.

The geologist claimed that the fire lit by the tourists had been kept alive by oil underground and he recommended that test-drilling be undertaken, but this was never done.

Portobello Gardens

Long before the construction of the Grand Canal or Portobello Harbour or the adjacent hotel, that general area on the road to Rathmines was known as Portobello. The district was generally believed to have been named to commemorate a battle which took place in Puerto Bello in the Gulf of Mexico in 1739 although some say that it was so named because Francis Drake had died in the same place in 1596.

Portobello House was one of five hotels built by the Grand Canal Company to accommodate passengers travelling to and from various locations along the canal. The hotel, which opened in July 1807, was taken over by the Sisters of Charity in 1860 and converted into a hospital for the blind until they moved to their present location at Merrion. Portobello House functioned as a private nursing home until 1971 and it now forms part of Portobello College.

Portobello Harbour was constructed in 1801 in order to provide moorings for the many 'fly boats' and barges using the canal. This picturesque little harbour was filled in in 1948 and a factory was built on the site.

Another feature of the district that has long since disappeared was the Royal Portobello Gardens, situated between Victoria Street off the South Circular Road and the Grand Canal. The gardens, which were then located in the suburbs of Dublin were a popular place of recreation with the local residents.

The park was opened in 1839 and throughout the course of the nineteenth century many events were held there, including fireworks displays, concerts, archery tournaments and sporting events. Other popular attractions included performing dogs, gymnastics and a group called the Hibernian Bell-ringers. The gardens even had their own horse-racing track and, on Easter Monday and Tuesday in 1859, Dublin newspapers gave notice of a race meeting to be held there followed by a fireworks display. The entrance fee was one shilling.

One of the last major events held in the Portobello gardens before its closure was a tightrope walk performed by the 'Great Blondin' in front of a huge crowd in 1861.

The gardens were sold soon afterwards to a property developer who built houses there in 1867.

Portobello Bridge built in 1791 was the scene of an appalling tragedy on the evening of 6 April 1861 when a horse-drawn omnibus toppled over into the locks drowning six passengers and two horses. The bus, which was travelling from Rathgar to Nelson's Pillar, had stopped on the steep bridge to allow two passengers to get off. When the driver tried to get the horses to resume the journey one of them became entangled in the reins. The horses were unable to move forward and the bus gradually pulled them back down the hill and into the lock dragging all six passengers and the two horses into the water below. A report from the *Freeman's Journal* of 8 April described what happened next:

> When the water was let off from the lock, so as to expose the top of the bus, Police Constable Gaffney and Private Smith of the 4th Light Dragoons got hatchets and with the aid of a ladder got on to the roof of the bus, broke a hole in the roof and took out the bodies. The lock depth was twenty-five feet, including ten of water. All the six passengers and the horses lost their lives. Any hopes of rescuing any of the passengers alive evaporated when in the confusion and panic, the lock-keeper opened the upper sluice-gates rather than the lower ones, filling the lock with even more water.

Fighting Fitz

One of the most active and violent men on the Dublin duelling scene in the eighteenth century was the Mayo-born Merrion Square resident, George Robert Fitzgerald, otherwise known as 'Mad, Fighting Fitzgerald'.

Fitzgerald, described by a contemporary as a 'reckless duellist' and 'a bold calculating murderer', loved to duel and he was said to have taken part in twenty-six showdowns before he had reached his twenty-sixth birthday. If a duelling partner wasn't readily available, George would prowl the streets of Dublin until he found one. He went out of his way to provoke fights, and he would often lash out at innocent passers-by in order to get a reaction. On one occasion he even shot off a man's wig in an attempt to get him to fight. He fought duels with Lord Norbury and Lord Clare and he once narrowly missed killing Denis Browne, a brother of Lord Altamont, when he fired a shot at him in the middle of Sackville Street.

Fitzgerald married Jane Connolly of Castletown in Kildare and helped her to spend her fortune while on an extended honeymoon of nearly three years, taking in Paris, Rome, Florence and Brussels. Fitz returned 'completely broke' and alone to his house at Merrion Square.

Fitzgerald was often at loggerheads with his own father over money matters and on one occasion he decided to teach the elder Fitzgerald a lesson by handcuffing him to a dancing bear for an entire day. Fitzgerald was later fined £500 and sentenced to two years' imprisonment at Castlebar

Gaol for this incident and for imprisoning the old man in a cave at the family home in Turlough.

He managed to obtain an early release from Castlebar when his friends rioted outside the gaol, but he was soon recaptured and thrown into Newgate Gaol in Dublin. He was pardoned after a few months, but he still suffered as a result of his confinement and it took him some time to recuperate at his house in Merrion Square.

Soon afterwards, Fitzgerald went to a play in the Crow Street Theatre in Temple Bar. Crow Street had a reputation for rowdiness and two soldiers with muskets and bayonets were deployed on both sides of the stage to keep order. Fitzgerald spotted one of his Mayo neighbours, 'Hair-Trigger Dick' Martin who had prosecuted him at his recent trial. Fitzgerald attacked Martin in the lobby of the theatre and the two had to be forcibly separated. Shortly afterwards, Martin sent a messenger over to Fitzgerald's house at Merrion Square to challenge him to a duel but Fitzgerald gave him an unmerciful beating with a large club. The duel eventually went ahead in Castlebar with both protagonists receiving only minor injuries. Martin refused to take part in a rematch, alleging that Fitzgerald had been wearing body armour during the first duel.

Fitzgerald was eventually tried and convicted for the murder of one of his neighbours and he was hanged at Castlebar for the crime on 12 June 1786. Before he was executed he drank a whole bottle of port and he threw himself off the scaffold. However, the rope snapped in two and Fitz fell onto the ground. He instructed the sheriff to go and get another rope – but not from the same shop. By the time a new rope had been procured, the effects of the port had begun to wear off and Fitzgerald lost his nerve and he spent his last moments on earth crying and praying for forgiveness for his crimes.

Theatre Royal

For several hundreds of years now, theatre-going and dramatic performances in general have been a major feature of Dublin's social scene. Medieval records show that performances were being put on by the guilds and churches of Dublin from as early as the fifteenth century on holy days and at festivals such as St George's Day and at the Feast of Corpus Christi.

Bands of strolling players were plying their trade in Dublin during the sixteenth century and in 1589 an entry in the *Ancient Treasury Book of Dublin* reveals that an amount of four pounds was paid to troupes called The Queen's Players and The Queen and Earl of Essex Players 'for showing their sports'.

In 1636 an attempt was made to regulate the numbers of wandering bands of actors and other 'rogues and vagabonds' who inhabited the streets of Dublin. During that year, an act of parliament passed in Dublin proclaimed that along with beggars, scam-artists, quacks and all other types of chancers, 'common players of interludes … jugglers and minstrels' were to be banned. Curiously, the act also allowed for the banning of those pretending 'to bee Egyptians, or wander in the habite, forme, or attire of counterfeit Egyptians'.

Dublin's first purpose-built theatre, known as The New Theatre, was erected at Werburgh Street in 1637 by a Scottish dancing master named John Ogilby, who later held the rather grandiose-sounding titles of 'Historiographer to his Majesty' and 'Master of the Revels in the Kingdom of Ireland'. The theatre was built just outside the walls of Dublin Castle and it was mainly patronised by members of the British nobility.

There are very few descriptions of the theatre in existence today, but one brief account furnished by a Thomas Wilkes states that it contained 'a gallery and pit, but no boxes, except one on the stage for the then lord deputy, the earl of Strafford, who was Ogilby's patron'. Another brief account contained in Robert Hitchcock's *An Historical View of the Irish Stage* says that the theatre was 'tolerably large and commodious'.

The theatre's first acting company and musicians were brought over from England at great expense by Ogilby and they produced many tragedies and comedies written by an English playwright named James Shirley, who was a friend of Ogilby's.

During the theatre's brief existence it never managed to attract spectators in sufficient numbers. In a desperate attempt to attract more punters Ogilby occasionally put on boxing matches, cudgelling, bear-baiting and cock-fighting contests at the theatre and these evenings seem to have been the only times that the theatre managed to attract capacity audiences. Bear and bull-baiting were very popular sports in Dublin at that time and there are many references in the Dublin newspapers to these practices. In 1639 the theatre was able to dispense with the bear-baiting when it had a great run of success with a play written by Henry Burnell called *Landgartha.*

Werburgh Street Theatre only lasted until 1641 when it was closed down during the Great Rebellion of that year. The theatre was closed by order of the puritanic lords justices and Ogilby – a royalist – fled to London, after having been almost killed in a gunpowder explosion at Rathfarnham Castle.

Ogilby returned to Dublin twenty years later and he built the famous Smock Alley Theatre in 1662. His second foray into the world of theatre was infinitely more successful than the first as Smock Alley remained open to theatre-goers for another 130 years.

Holy Wells

The practice of visiting holy wells or springs in some cases extends back to pre-Christian times and nearly 200 of these have been recorded in the greater Dublin area. A great many of these wells have long since disappeared from public view.

The annual feast day of St John the Baptist on 24 June was an important festival for many years in Dublin. Bonfires were lit and maintained throughout the entire night. These bonfires were very popular in Dublin and they were often banned because of the danger caused to the wooden houses of the city.

Thousands gathered annually at St John's Well to partake of the waters, which were said to cure all manner of diseases. This well was located near Islandbridge in the vicinity of what is now St John's Terrace near Kilmainham. This well was famous for its curative powers and over the course of many centuries it attracted pilgrims in their thousands. As the years went by, the annual festival became bigger and more unruly and, like so many other festivals in the city, drinking and rioting became its main focus.

Throughout the eighteenth century many festivals were banned because of the public nuisance caused and the annual visit to St John's Well was no different. In 1710 the Irish House of Commons passed an act which allowed for punishment by fines, floggings or imprisonment for those engaged in 'dangerous, tumultuous and unlawful assemblies'. The act led to the cancellation of the festival for a few years, although it does appear that the religious aspect of the day was still observed by many. Twenty-five years later the owners of the nearby Royal Hospital in Kilmainham complained about damage caused to their property by the large numbers of visitors to the well who used the grounds of the Royal Hospital as a shortcut.

One famous well still in existence is Lady's Well at Mulhuddart. This well is reputed to aid in the healing of cuts, sprains and bruises. This well attracted the attention of the authorities during the eighteenth century for all the wrong reasons and the local Catholic church tried to bring a halt to the drink-fuelled revelry that took place there every September.

Some weeks before the festivities were due to take place in 1754 a report in *Faulkner's Dublin Journal* warned publicans not to turn up on the day:

> We are assured that the Roman Catholic clergy, to prevent as far as in them lieth, the enormities and scandalous excesses that are annually committed at the Well near Mulahedard, commonly called Lady's Well, have prevailed on the landholders contigious thereto not to permit any tents or booths to be erected hereafter on their lands; of which it is judged proper to give notice in this publick manner, to prevent a disappointment to such publicans as usually erected tents or booths near said Well.

Another famous well was St Brigid's Well at St Margaret's in north county Dublin. This well was said to be particularly cool in summer and was reputed never to freeze over in winter. There was another well dedicated to St Patrick near Finglas village. This well was popular with people suffering from blindness and other eye problems and it was claimed that drinking the water was a good cure for ulcers.

The Spa Well beside the Spa Hotel in Lucan also had a great reputation for its restorative properties and was believed to cure, amongst other ailments: ringworm, cold-sores, rheumatism, loose teeth, leprosy and even paralysis. During the eighteenth century, the water was even bottled and brought to Dr Stevens' Hospital where it was used to treat ulcers. Dr John Rutty, in his *Natural History of Ireland* said that the water 'tasted of a boiled egg ... and smelt like a solution of sulphur'.

Old Newgate Prison

Its not known exactly when the old Newgate gaol which stood on the corner of Cut Purse Row and Lamb Alley was built but it is first mentioned as a place of confinement in 1285. The prison was called Newgate because it was built on the site of the western gate of the old city walls. The prison was described as consisting of a round tower at each corner, an iron gate and portcullis. It also contained an iron balcony that was used for public hangings.

According to Gilbert's *History of Dublin* the building became the main city prison in 1485 after Richard III had authorised the mayor and sheriffs of Dublin to maintain a gaol in the city. However, this doesn't mean that Newgate was the first gaol in the city as there had previously been one near the city wall between Dublin Castle and Werburgh Street.

According to an entry in the *Chain Book of Dublin* in 1486 (so called because it was chained to a wall in the Tholsel to stop citizens from running away with it), the mayor of Dublin, Janico Marks, and his two bailiffs, Thomas Bennet and Robert Blanchville, took delivery of the following iron instruments to be used in the prison: three shears, two keys, two bolts with three collars, one three-pointed bolt for men's hands, shackles for men's legs, one great chain weighing eight and a half stone, yokes with collars, one pair of manacles weighing one stone, stock-locks, two hanging-locks and a variety of other collars and shackles.

Another inventory drawn up in 1526 lists the following: four bolts for men's legs with their shackles, one bolt for children with two shackles, collars for men's necks, keys for both dungeons beneath and a tool called a clinching hammer.

The inventory also reveals that there were seven prisoners incarcerated in Newgate at that time. Four were in for non-payment of debts, two of the prisoners – Leonard Cantwell and Richard Kelly – were being held for felony while one, Bell Brysse, was there for trespass.

In 1534 the head gaoler of Newgate, Dick Stanton, is mentioned in *Hollinshed's Chronicles* for defending Newgate during an attack by rebels loyal to Silken Thomas. According to the book, Stanton saw one of the rebels pointing his musket in the window of Newgate so he shot him 'full in the forehead under the brim of his skull and withal turned up his heeles. Stanton, not satisfied with his death, issued out of the wicket, stript the varlet mother naked and brought in his piece and attire ...'

The gaolers at Newgate were appointed by the Dublin City Assembly and they received little or no remuneration from the authorities for the privilege. They were also expected to pay for the upkeep and maintenance of Newgate. The gaolers did manage to earn a substantial living by extorting money from the prisoners in their charge. The unfortunate inmates of the prison were forced to pay for everything including food, drink and even a dry mattress to sleep on. The gaoler could also boost his income by selling alcohol to the prisoners at grossly inflated prices.

In 1729, the Irish House of Commons instigated an inquiry into the behaviour of John Hawkins who was gaoler of Newgate and the adjoining Black Dog Prison. Hawkins required every prisoner who came through the gates of the prisons to pay two shillings into a 'penny pot'. Those who refused were stripped and beaten by Hawkins' henchmen who would then sell the inmates' clothes for the penny pot. Any prisoner unable to pay bed rent was thrown into a small, damp and windowless dungeon called 'The Nunnery' which could sometimes hold up to twenty prisoners.

Hawkins even entered into an arrangement with the parish watch whereby they would arrest completely innocent people at their homes and take them to straight to Newgate where Hawkins would often detain them for days on end until they could come up with the required release fee. The committee investigating the abuses at the prison established that of the 160 prisoners in Newgate at the time, only forty of them were actually awaiting trial!

Throughout the seventeenth and eighteenth centuries, Newgate had to undergo several renovations and in 1773 a decision was taken to abandon the prison and build a new Newgate across the Liffey at Green Street. The new prison opened for business in 1780 but the old Newgate continued to be used until 1782 when the City Assembly ordered that 'the old building at Cornmarket, commonly called Newgate, should be immediately pulled down, the same being a nuisance and that a message be sent to the Lord

Mayor and Board of Aldermen requesting their concurrence therewith'.

The mayor concurred and the old Newgate Prison was demolished in August 1782.

Simpson's Hospital

During the 1770s a Jervis Street merchant named George Simpson – who was also a chronic gout sufferer – decided to set up an institution for poor Dublin men who were in a similar situation. Simpson died in 1778 leaving a small fortune and in his will he directed that after the death of his wife Catherine, his fortune was to be used 'to erect and support and maintain, an hospital for the reception of such poor decayed, blind and gouty men as they shall think worthy of such a charity'.

Catherine followed her husband to the grave soon afterwards and a committee of thirteen men – all friends of Simpson – was appointed to administer his last wishes. A large number of local charities and institutions benefited from Simpson's generosity and in 1781, Simpson's hospital for 'blind and gouty old men' eventually opened at Putland House on Parnell Street, then Great Britain Street close to where the Ilac Centre is now situated. This house was demolished a short time later and a new hospital was in place on the site by 1787.

This building was described by Samuel Lewis' *Topographical Dictionary of Ireland* in 1837 as being 'a large plain building, with a small plot of ground in the rear for the accommodation of the inmates: its interior is divided into twenty-four wards, containing about seventy beds, but the number supported is about fifty'.

The inmates of Simpson's hospital were a familiar and easily recognisable sight on the streets of Dublin with their distinctive uniforms, which consisted of a black felt top hat, a pilot-blue suit and walking cane.

There were landscaped gardens at the back of the hospital where the residents could stroll along gravelled walkways or smoke their pipes on one of the wooden benches provided for their comfort. A contemporary visitor to the hospital described the garden as a peaceful haven from the bustle of the city saying: 'In the spring and summer the gay sound of the flute and violin is often heard from the benches of their little garden, and the whole institution has an air of cheerful content.'

The hospital was transferred to more suitable premises at Wyckham in Dundrum in 1925 and it is still in use as a home for the elderly. The old hospital building in Parnell Street was taken over by a company named Williams and Woods who built a factory on the site of the old gardens at the back of the premises. This was demolished in 1978.

Also located in Parnell Street was St Mary's or the Widows Alms House, which was established in 1724. This charitable institution was established to provide food and lodgings for thirty-two destitute widows of St Mary's parish. The alms house initially catered for children too but the trustees decided that this was an unsuitable place to look after their welfare.

The widows were given a room measuring fourteen feet by twelve with a fireplace and a weekly allowance of bread, coal and candles and in some cases, a small allowance.

Warburton, Walsh and Whitelaw's *History of the City of Dublin* written in 1818 painted a grim picture of the house in which a 'general character of gloom and dirt pervades every room'. They described walls streaked with dirt and smoke, windows so filthy that no daylight could shine through them and a rotting roof that was just about ready to collapse on the unfortunate inmates below.

The house was still in use during the 1950s and like Simpson's hospital it was demolished during the 1970s.

State Coach

In recent years Dublin's lord mayors have been reasonably well looked after in transport terms compared to their counterparts of 300 years ago. Most of today's mayors are now provided with a set of wheels and a driver to ferry them around the city to carry out their duties, while some have even been known to resort to the bicycle on occasion.

However, up until 1791 Dublin Corporation had no state coach and the lord mayor either had to provide his own transport or else walk to civic functions. For instance, can you imagine the embarrassment of the lord mayor in 1701 when he was forced to walk behind the carriages of the lords justice to the unveiling of a statue to King Billy

(William of Orange) on College Green, because he had no coach of his own?

Things were slightly better for Lord Mayor Humphrey French in 1732 who made what *Pue's Occurrences* described as 'the greatest appearance that was ever known on such an occasion' at King George II's birthday bash in October of that year. French's coach was pulled by six horses and was manned by several elaborately dressed footmen. However, French was a man of independent means and he provided the coach himself.

Nearly twenty years later Lord Mayor French was back on shanks mare again and the newspapers reported in July 1751 that he walked from the Tholsel in High Street to lay the foundation stone of the new Rotunda hospital in what was then Great Britain Street.

The City Assembly did toy with the idea of buying a coach in 1763 but nothing further was done about it. Three years later the problem was solved by the duke of Leinster who donated a 'Berlin' coach to the city of Dublin. This coach was in use for twenty years but it became too costly to keep it in a decent state of repair. Just before it was scrapped altogether, a member of the Assembly, John 'The Dog in Office' Gifford, said that if £50 was spent on the carriage, it still wouldn't be worth £15.

In 1789 the corporation decided that a new coach should be built and William Whitton, a Dominick Street coach-builder, won the contract. There were at least thirty coach-building firms in the city at that time – mostly on the north side.

Whitton began the building of the coach using the best artists and craftsmen available to him and it was ready for use by November 1790. However, just before the coach was due to be displayed to the public, the lord chancellor, Lord Clare's London-built coach costing £7,000 appeared on the streets of Dublin. The corporation was determined to show that anything London could do, they could do better and they decided to redesign the state coach. The new improved Dublin coach appeared on the streets one year later just in time for the celebration of William of Orange's birthday. Unlike ninety years earlier, the lord mayor didn't have to walk to the party. King Billy would have been pleased too as on each corner of the roof of the coach was a carved figure of a child carrying bunches of orange lilies, which, said a contemporary description, 'reminds us of William III who delivered these countries from a Popish tyrant.' The Dublin coach cost a total of £2,690 to build, less than half the cost of its London rival.

During the latter part of the eighteenth century the state coach was only used sporadically and it made a rare appearance at the Eucharistic Congress in 1932. The coach reappeared in 1976 after it was completely restored by Dublin Corporation and it has remained an annual feature of the St Patrick's Day parade ever since.

Lundy Foot

Today, the remains of Lundy Foot, a well-known Dublin snuff and tobacco manufacturer, lie buried in St Matthew's churchyard in Irishtown. Foot's tobacco shop stood at the junction of Westmoreland Street and D'Olier Street facing O'Connell Bridge and he also had a factory at the corner of Parliament Street and Essex Gate.

Foot lived in a house called Footmount at the bottom of Mount Pelier just below the Hell Fire Club and he built the house, which is now an Augustinian retreat centre, in 1790.

Foot came from an extremely wealthy family and, in addition to working in the family business, he also studied law. He was called to the bar in 1788 at the age of twenty-four and he later became a magistrate. He was extremely unpopular in this capacity and he was renowned for his over-enthusiastic sentencing policy.

Foot is chiefly remembered today for his conviction of three members of the Kearney family from Piperstown in 1816 for the murder of Ponsonby Shaw's land steward, John Kinlan, at Bohernabreena.

Kinlan was an unpopular man in the area and he was also known to be an informer, so when he disappeared one night in 1816 no one in the locality was too upset. Although Kinlan's body was never found, the Kearneys were arrested and charged with murder. The Kearneys had apparently been heard to utter threats against the land steward and an axe with blood and human hair was discovered. This 'evidence' was purely circumstantial but Foot convicted the three men on a charge of conspiracy to murder and sentenced them to death.

The three men, Peter, Joe and Billy Kearney, were taken from Kilmainham Jail in a cart and they were brought to their place of execution on the banks of the Dodder near Old Bawn in Tallaght. When they passed the Shaw family home at Bushy Park in Terenure, the men asked for the cart to be stopped for a minute. The Kearneys then knelt down in the cart and cursed the seed and breed of the Shaw family for all eternity and then went on their way to their place of execution.

An eyewitness to the hanging said that the men were hanged on a triangular shaped scaffold. One son climbed up the ladder first and helped his father and he was followed up by the other son. At that point another Kearney brother, who hadn't been implicated in the crime stepped forward from the crowd and asked to take his father's place on the scaffold. This request was refused and, according to the witness: 'The three of them were hanged together, and the bodies were then thrown into a cart and brought back to Dublin.'

Foot later sold his house at Orlagh and moved to Rosbercon Castle in New Ross. On 2 January 1835 Foot, who was by then seventy years of age, was attacked near his home and bludgeoned to death with a large stone. At the time there was wild speculation that members of the Kearney family had taken their revenge on Foot but the real culprit was soon unmasked.

Foot had bought a small landholding that had previously been worked by an evicted tenant named Murphy. Murphy's son James was seen fleeing from the scene of the attack and he was convicted of murder and hanged.

Lundy Foot was initially buried in Kilkenny but his remains were moved later to the family tomb at St Matthew's in Irishtown.

Mount Jerome

Mount Jerome Cemetery in Harold's Cross takes its name from a Reverend Stephen Jerome who was vicar of St Kevin's parish just before the outbreak of the rebellion of 1641. At the time, Jerome was well known around Dublin for his 'fire and brimstone' style of preaching and after the rebellion had been put down he was, according to Elrington Ball, 'appointed a special preacher of St Patrick's Cathedral to stir up the devotion of the congregation and to instruct the soldiers in those times and brought on himself the censure of the Irish House of Lords by his advocacy of Puritan opinions'.

In later years the lands were owned by the earl of Meath. The original house built during the eighteenth century on the Mount Jerome estate is now used as a cemetery office. Three hundred years ago this house was owned by the Falkiner family and in 1784 the house had been leased by John Keogh, a leading light in the movement for Catholic emancipation. Keogh lived at Mount Jerome until his death in 1817 and in 1834 his family sold the house and lands to the Dublin General Cemetery Company.

The cemetery opened just in time for inclusion in Samuel Lewis' *Topographical Dictionary of Ireland* , first published in 1837, and it provides some interesting information on the cemetery. Lewis described Mount Jerome as 'a beautifully picturesque demesne' consisting of 'twenty-five acres of gently elevated ground, embellished with lawns and shrubberies, and wholly surrounded with lofty trees of venerable growth, giving it an air of seclusion and a solemnity of aspect peculiarly appropriate'.

The Dublin Cemetery Company was set up as a profit-making concern with an initial stake of £12,000. It was initially envisaged that people of all religions would be buried at Mount Jerome, but Catholics weren't buried there until the 1920s when Glasnevin cemetery was temporarily closed during a strike.

The company entered into an agreement with the owners of the Grand Canal for the improvement of the road leading from Portobello to the cemetery, and all hearses travelling to and from Mount Jerome were exempted from paying a toll that was then in force. The Dublin Cemetery Company went into liquidation in 1983 and the cemetery was sold to Massey's undertakers in 1984.

The cemetery is laid out in a series of walkways with names such as the Nun's Walk, Orphan's Walk, Guinness Walk and Consecration Walk, and the remains of scores of Ireland's best-known painters, playwrights, patriots, peelers and others are interred there.

There is a plot for deceased members of the Royal Irish Constabulary and the Dublin Metropolitan Police, and a large number of members of Dublin's Huguenot community were re-buried at Mount Jerome following the closure of the Huguenot cemetery at Peter Street.

There are some unusual monuments in Mount Jerome including the Harvie Memorial which features the statue of a dog. The statue had been headless for many years but the head has recently been restored by the owners of the cemetery. Apparently the dog had made a vain attempt to save his owner from drowning and both dog and master were buried in the same grave.

Another unusual monument close by is the Gresham family vault. This was the tomb of a woman who was afraid of being buried alive and the coffin had a spring-locked lid just in case she wasn't really dead. There was also a bell inside the tomb that she could ring to attract the attention of passersby.

Roomkeeper's Society

Way back in 1790, long before the advent of the welfare state, the Sick and Indigent Roomkeeper's Society was established to give aid to Dubliners who had fallen on hard times through no fault of their own. The society was only set up to look after those who were unable to work or families who had lost their main breadwinner. Aid was given on a temporary basis and usually took the form of help with rent arrears, and sometimes tools or equipment were given to people in order to help them to provide for themselves.

The society was founded in a room in Mountrath Street on 15 March 1790 and the nine-man committee consisted of several merchants, a carpenter, a stonecutter and a fruit seller. The committee decided that members should contribute two pence per week toward a fund for the relief of 'persons who had never begged abroad, industrious mechanics and indigent roomkeepers who, above all others are the most pitiable objects of distress'.

The society was, unusually for its time, a non-sectarian, non-denominational organisation and it often went to great lengths to emphasise this virtue. They even went so far as to change the name of the society in 1799 to 'The Charitable Society for the Relief of the Sick and Indigent Roomkeepers of all Religious Persuasions in the City of Dublin'.

The leading light of the society was a man called Samuel Roseburgh who was one of the original founders of the charity. Roseburgh, a linen draper, was involved with the Roomkeepers for over forty years and he explained in a pamphlet written in 1801 his reasons for getting involved:

> I have often reflected on the situation of a poor man or woman walking about our streets the entire day with little or no clothing to cover them and the little they have in rags. I have followed them to their miserable retreats and found their accommodation inferior to that of a brute.'

The society used a variety of methods to raise funds including the staging of an annual ball, subscriptions and charity sermons. The annual ball seems to have run into trouble during the latter part of the nineteenth century and in 1864 the lord lieutenant refused to attend the ball 'due to the admission of improper characters which of late years was increasing.' The annual ball was again a point of contention in 1877 when the archbishop of Dublin and three other committee members resigned from the society. It emerged later that the men had objected to high jinks that had taken place at the ball and they made an intriguing reference to 'men appearing in female attire'. Soon afterwards, the annual ball was replaced by a temperance picnic.

During its earliest days, the society met in coffee houses and pubs such as Mulligans in Poolbeg Street and in 1855 the society bought a house at 2 Palace Street in the shadow of Dublin Castle (opposite the Olympia Theatre) with the help of a donation from Benjamin Lee Guinness. The Sick and Indigent Roomkeeper's Society left this wonderful old building during the early 1990s and it remains as a focal point for Dubliners and visitors alike.

The work begun by Samuel Roseburgh and his friends in 1790 still continues today and the Sick and Indigent Roomkeeper's Society is still in business at 34 Lower Leeson Street, which makes it Dublin's, if not Ireland's, oldest and longest running charity.

Bullock Harbour

Between the villages of Sandycove and Dalkey lies the picturesque Bullock harbour and castle. Nowadays, the harbour is a nice place to spend a summer's evening but in former times Bullock was a thriving and prosperous place with an identity all of its own.

In pre-Norman times Bullock or 'Bloyke' belonged to the monks of St Mary's Abbey in Dublin and they also controlled fishing rights in the harbour. In 1346, local fishermen brought an action against the abbot of Bloyke for stealing their fish.

However, the courts decided that the abbot was perfectly within his rights and ordered that henceforth the monks were entitled to have one fish from every catch landed at Bullock and an annual tax of 600 fish from every herring boat fishing out of the harbour. The impressive Bullock Castle was built by the monks in order to protect their fishing interests which grew to a considerable size in medieval times. The castle and the lands immediately surrounding it were in a vulnerable position due to its location on the border of the Pale, and the settlement was attacked many times throughout the years.

One of the first recorded attacks on Bloyke occurred in 1312 when raiders described as 'enemies of the king' made off with a large consignment of corn and other items belonging to the monks.

Following the dissolution of the monasteries in 1539 Bloyke, which then contained two houses and six cottages in addition to the castle, was described as a strongly defended and walled settlement partly covered by fir trees.

In 1542, Bloyke was leased out to a number of families loyal to the Crown, including the Talbots and later on the Fagan family. In 1611, while under the ownership of John Fagan, the settlement – although the castle appeared to be in bad shape – had grown substantially and John Dalton in his *History of the County of Dublin* says that it contained along with the castle and a tumbledown tower, 'thirty dwelling-houses, 10 acres of meadow, 200 acres of pasture and furze, with the fishing and haven to the main sea'. It had grown to such an extent 150 years later that one contemporary writer described it as 'a complete walled town in miniature'.

Down through the ages Bullock Harbour was a popular haunt of smugglers and there have been many tales recorded in relation to conflict between them and the customs men.

The *Dublin Weekly Journal* of 25 April 1735 reported on a major incident at Bullock in which two smugglers were killed by the revenue men: 'Last week some of the King's officers made a seizure of a large quantity of tea and brandy at Bullock, and next morning several persons attempted to rescue it from the officers, which occasioned a great battle, in which several were wounded on both sides; one Mr Brown, an officer, was shot through the thigh, and 'tis thought two of the smugglers were killed.'

The current harbour at Bullock was built on the site of the medieval pier nearly two hundred years ago when the Dublin Ballast Board – forerunner of the Dublin Port Authority – acquired the leases on land at Bullock for quarrying purposes in 1804. A local contractor, George Smith, was awarded the contract for the quarrying of the stone and the construction of the new harbour in 1819. The harbour was, for a period of time, used as a base for Dublin pilot boats operating in Dublin Bay, and a number of cottages were built for the accommodation of the pilots at a cost of £10 each. A lifeboat was stationed at Bullock during the same period, but it could only be used when the weather was fine.

Dunlop

Today, millions of cyclists and motorists worldwide all take for granted the air-filled rubber tyres and tubes that propel them with relative ease on their journeys. However, before their invention in 1888, cycling was an altogether different and very uncomfortable experience. The earliest tyres were manufactured from leather and later on they were made of solid rubber.

A plaque on the wall of a building in Dublin's Upper Stephen Street is now the only visible reminder that the world's first tyre factory was located here. It reads: 'The first pneumatic tyre factory in the world was started here in 1889 to make tyres under John Boyd Dunlop's patent of 7 December 1888.'

John Boyd Dunlop, a Scottish Belfast-based veterinary surgeon has been widely credited as the inventor of the pneumatic tyre as we now know it. There had been an earlier version of the pneumatic tyre invented by another Scot – Robert Thomson – in 1845 but it was before its time and it was never developed commercially.

From an early age Dunlop, as he said himself in his *History of the Pneumatic Tyre*, had developed an interest in the improvement of all types of locomotion 'by road, rail and sea'.

It gradually dawned on Dunlop that he could make travel by bicycle faster and more comfortable by adding a tube made from rubber and canvas and filled with compressed air.

Dunlop first came up with the concept of the pneumatic tyre when he observed that his son Johnnie's bicycle was subjected to a tremendous amount of shaking as he cycled it around the cobbled streets of Belfast.

Dunlop decided to have a go at improving the solid rubber tyre and his first experiment involved the fixing of a tube made from a sheet of rubber to a circular wooden disc. He then inflated the tube with his son's football pump and sealed the tube by tying it off at both ends. The tube was then secured to the disc by nailing a canvas strip all around the edge.

Dunlop then tested his new invention by rolling it along the length of his stable yard and he saw that it travelled much further and faster than Johnnie's solid wheel. Dunlop made further modifications to the wheel and he came up with the idea of using a rubber tyre instead of the canvas.

Dunlop applied for a patent for his idea on 23 July 1888 and it was to all intents and purposes the world's first pneumatic tyre. Within six months, Dunlop's new invention was being used on the cycling track at Queen's University in Belfast and it began to attract widespread interest.

In 1889, a group of Dublin businessmen who realised the importance of Dunlop's invention approached him with a view to forming a company and the Pneumatic Tyre and Booth's Cycle Agency came into being later that year. The company's headquarters were at Upper Stephen's Street, while manufacturing operations were carried out at 35 Westland Row.

However, Dublin's connection with the emerging tyre industry was severed during that year when the company decided to shift its entire operation to Coventry. This followed a court case taken against it by Dublin Corporation because of pollution caused by the manufacture of the tyres at Westland Row.

Dunlop came to live in Dublin on a permanent basis in April 1892 and he took up residence at Mount Merrion and then 46 Ailesbury Road where he lived for the remainder of his life. He resigned as a director from the Pneumatic Tyre Company and Booths Cycle Agency in 1895 and sold the bulk of his shares in the company.

John Boyd Dunlop, the man whose invention revolutionised the bicycle and motor car, died on 23 October 1921 and is buried in Deansgrange Cemetery.

Art's Escape

A recent trip to the reputed last resting place of Art O'Neill deep in the heart of the Wicklow Mountains called to mind an epic escape from Dublin Castle over 400 years ago.

Every year, as close to midnight on 'Little Christmas', 6 January, as they can manage it, a group of intrepid walkers set off from the walls of Dublin Castle in commemoration of the great escape from Dublin Castle of Red Hugh O'Donnell and Art O'Neill on 6 January 1592.

The 53 kilometre walk follows the route taken by O'Neill and O'Donnell, who were attempting to reach the safety of Fiach McHugh O'Byrne's mountain stronghold at Glenmalure in Wicklow.

The fifteen-year-old Red Hugh O'Donnell had been kidnapped some five years earlier when the English lord deputy, John Perrot, lured him on board a ship at Rathmullan in Donegal and took him to Dublin, where he was held in an effort to secure his father's compliance with the English administration in Ireland.

O'Donnell had attempted an escape from the Gate Tower of Dublin Castle one year earlier in 1591 when he and a number of companions smuggled a rope into the castle. O'Donnell actually managed to reach Felim O'Toole's territory in Wicklow but O'Toole, fearing retribution from the English, brought him back to Dublin.

O'Donnell was then confined in chains in the castle's Record Tower, where he was placed under heavy guard. Despite the increased security O'Donnell managed to escape again one year later.

Red Hugh along with Art and Henry O'Neill managed to overpower their gaolers and they escaped by sliding down what the transcriber of the annals politely described as 'privy-chutes' but were really open sewage pipes.

Once the three men had safely negotiated the deep defensive ditch that then surrounded Dublin Castle they were met by a guide, who brought them safely away from the city and into the foothills of the Dublin mountains, where they separated from Henry O'Neill.

However, the men made slow progress because Art – who had grown heavy in prison – was so weak that Red Hugh and the guide were forced to carry him. Their progress was hindered further by the cold January weather. It was snowing that night and the men were only lightly clothed as they had been forced to leave their heavy cloaks behind.

The men's destination on that occasion was the Glenmalure fortress of Fiach McHugh O'Byrne, but they were forced to seek shelter at the bottom of a cliff near a place now known as Glenreemore (the 'glen of the big king').

Hugh sent the guide on to O'Byrne's stronghold for help. Fiach immediately sent some of his servants to help the men and bring them food, ale and beer but when they eventually found Art and Red Hugh, the two men were unconscious and covered with snow and hailstones. Fiach's men did their best to revive them but Art died soon afterwards from exposure and was buried there. Red Hugh, suffering from frostbite, was carried to Glenmalure where he laid low until he had sufficiently recovered to make his way back to Donegal.

On his return to Ballyshannon, Red Hugh had both of his frost-bitten toes amputated. He eventually succeeded his father as leader of the O'Donnells and during the following years he became the main ally of the earl of Tyrone, Hugh O'Neill. Following the Battle of Kinsale in 1601, O'Donnell fled to Spain where he died in 1602.

Bishop Whateley

During the mid-eighteenth century the Protestant archbishop of Dublin, Richard Whateley, was a familiar sight on the south-side streets of Dublin. Besides being a man of the cloth, Whateley was also an economist, philosopher and ardent social reformer. He was also a vociferous supporter of Catholic emancipation and he campaigned extensively for the abolition of transportation of Irish prisoners to British colonies throughout the New World.

Whateley, the son of a Bristol cleric, was born in 1787 and he was said to have been an extremely absent-minded child. So much so that he was totally unaware of the names of streets and shops in his own locality. He was sent to Oxford at the age of eighteen and he later became a don there. During his time at Oxford Whateley was known as a controversial liberal and a progressive thinker and he attracted large crowds to his sermons. Even during those early years Whateley was renowned for being extremely restless and many attended his sermons simply to see what antics he would get up to.

In 1831 he was sent to Dublin as archbishop by the English Whig prime minister Lord Grey, who felt that Dubliners might appreciate his down-to-earth qualities a bit more than those of his stuffier predecessors.

These qualities weren't immediately obvious to members of his own church and the often controversial and outspoken Whateley seems to have made several enemies within its ranks for working too closely with Catholics on a common religious curriculum. In his *Memoirs of Richard Whateley* written in 1864, W.J. Fitzpatrick gives details of a confrontation between the archbishop and one of his critics. 'Pray sir,' said the archbishop, 'why are you like the bell of your own church steeple?' The clergyman thought for a moment before replying, 'Because I am always ready to sound the alarm when the church is in danger.'

'No,' said Whateley, 'it is because you have an empty head and a long tongue.'

Dubliners must have been more than a little bemused with their new archbishop's behaviour as he was often seen sitting on the fence outside his palace at 16 St Stephen's Green smoking his pipe or playing in the palace gardens with his boomerang. On other occasions he would be seen climbing trees on the green or playing hide-and-seek with his dogs and he was even observed stoning crows there on occasion.

Whateley was never happier than when he was in his garden and it must have been a peculiar sight to see him wandering through it on his twice-daily walks dressed in his old vestments while slashing at weeds with his walking stick with a large steel blade attached to the end of it.

The archbishop had many peculiar habits which included paring his nails at the dinner table and he often alarmed his fellow diners by twirling his chair around on one leg at top speed. He often attended meetings of the National Board of Education at Antrim House in Merrion Square, where he managed to wear a large hole in the carpet by swinging on his chair. The hole was referred to for many years afterwards as 'Whateley's Hole'.

Whateley's wife of nearly forty years died in 1860 and Whateley was overcome with grief. He became gravely ill and he rejected all attempts to help him, even to the extent of throwing his medicine out the window. He eventually died from a stroke in 1863 at the age of seventy-seven.

Zozimus

Michael Moran a.k.a Zozimus was born in Faddle Alley near Blackpitts in the Liberties sometime around 1794 and as far as Dublin 'characters' go, Zoz was the granddaddy of them all. He took the name Zozimus from one his favourite recitations, which told the story of a meeting in the desert between St Mary of Egypt and Zozimus, a fifth-century holy man.

Moran, who was blind almost from birth, won fame in the city from an early age as a ballad-maker, raconteur and reciter. During his early years he was only one of a number of roving minstrels in the city and he learned his trade from the likes of the Winetavern Street balladeer, Brady the tanner's son, and the two Richards – Madden and Shiel – who were both weavers from the Liberties, and Reynolds the poet who was renowned for his savage wit and sarcasm.

Zoz's strengths lay in his recitations and he was often seen on his rounds dressed in what his biographer described as a long frieze coat, a greasy brown beaver hat, corduroy trousers and a pair of 'strong Francis Street brogues.' He also carried a large blackthorn stick attached to his wrist with a leather strap.

Zoz had a regular beat and each day of the week would see him in a different part of the city. Sometimes he took up position at the top of Grafton Street or on Dame Street or Henry Street or his favourite pitch on Carlisle Bridge (now O'Connell Bridge).

Zozimus fell foul of the law on many occasions and he

had several encounters with one member of the Dublin Metropolitan Police force in particular. DMP constable 184B had a particular dislike for ballad-singers and street performers and the blind Zozimus was at the top of his hit list. 184B didn't like the press either and he made the mistake of hassling a journalist named Dunphy who worked for the *Freeman's Journal*.

The disgruntled hacks and street entertainers soon joined forces to get even with 184B with the result that he was lampooned and ridiculed in newspaper articles and by every ballad-singer in the city. 184B became so famous that tourists went out of their way to come to Dublin to take a look at him. Wherever 184B went he was followed by crowds of Dubliners who would hurl abuse at him and laugh at his every move. Eventually, his position became untenable and he was removed from the force. For many years afterwards no other constable would wear the number 184B for fear of receiving the same treatment.

Of course, Zozimus was only too glad to join in the vilification of 184B and he wrote a ballad that was simply entitled '184B', which concluded with the verse:

How proud Robert Peel must be of such a chap,
He stands about five feet nothing in cap,
And his name's immortalized by his friend Mr D,
A statue must be riz to 184B.

(Mr D. is a reference to the journalist Dunphy.)

Zozimus died following a short illness on 3 April 1846 at his home in Patrick Street and he was buried in an unmarked pauper's grave at Glasnevin although a memorial was erected over the plot in 1988. Zozimus had asked to be buried in the better-protected Glasnevin cemetery after his friend Stoney Pockets' remains had been taken by body snatchers from Merrion churchyard.

Walking Gallows

In his *Personal Sketches of His Own Times* published in 1830 Jonah Barrington provides us with a sketch of one Lieutenant Edward Hepenstall, one of the most feared loyalist militiamen of 1798. Barrington, who knew Hepenstall personally, described him as a large and extremely powerful man but one 'so cold-blooded and so eccentric an executioner of the human race I believe never yet existed, save among the American Indians'.

Hepenstall, who was a lieutenant in the County Wicklow Militia, was born at Newcastle in County Wicklow sometime around 1766 and was known on the streets of Dublin and the greater Leinster area as 'Walking Gallows'.

Walking Gallows earned his nickname because he hanged so many Irishmen whom he believed to be rebels on his own back, literally. He acted as judge, jury and executioner and he would often hang those he suspected as being rebels on the flimsiest of evidence.

Hepenstall developed a barbarous method of executing his victims by twisting his scarf into a makeshift loop and sliding it over the condemned man's neck. He would then pull the other end of the scarf over his own shoulder and set off at a run with the unfortunate victim jolting on his back, strangling him in the process. Hepenstall would then give the dying man a parting twist of the scarf to make sure he was dead before handing him over to his aide-de-camp for disposal.

W.J. Fitzpatrick gave a similar description of Walking Gallows in his book entitled *The Sham Squire and The Informers of 1798*: 'If Hepenstall met a peasant who could not satisfactorily account for himself, he knocked him down with a blow from his fist, which was quite effectual as a sledge-hammer, and then adjusting a noose round the prisoner's neck, drew the rope over his own shoulders, and trotted about, the victim's legs dangling in the air, and his tongue protruding, until death at last put an end to the torture.'

According to Barrington, Hepenstall carried out many of his Dublin executions at a place he calls the 'commercial exchange of Dublin' which could have been one of two places: the place now covered by the Commercial Buildings at College Green or the Royal Exchange, now called City Hall.

Hepenstall is also known to have carried out at least one execution in a stable yard at the rear of Kerry House on St Stephen's Green. Barrington seemed to think that this particular execution was justified because 'the hangee' on that occasion turned out to be a real rebel.

The time and place of Walking Gallows' own death has been the subject of much disagreement over the years.

Watty Cox's *Irish Magazine* claimed that Hepenstall died in great pain at his brother's house at Andrews Street in 1804, while an entry in the Sham Squire Francis Higgins' diary on 18 September 1800 reads: 'Died on Thursday night, of a dropsical complaint. Lieutenant Edward Hepenstall, of the 68th Regiment, sometime back an officer in the Wicklow militia – a gentleman whose intrepidity and spirit during the Rebellion rendered much general good.'

Higgins also claims that Hepenstall was buried at St Andrew's churchyard in an unmarked grave and it was suggested that his headstone should contain an inscription with just two lines:

Here lies the bones of Hepenstall,
Judge, jury, gallows, rope and all.

We'll leave the last word on Walking Gallows to Jonah Barrington who speculated on the possible whereabouts of Hepenstall's ghost:

He may be employed somewhere else in the very same way wherein he entertained himself in Ireland; and that after being duly furnished with a tail, horns, and cloven foot, no spirit could do better business than the lieutenant.

Martello Towers

A Dublin newspaper report of September 1804 heralded the appearance of some of Dublin's best-known coastal landmarks: 'The building of the Martello towers for the protection of the coast from Bray to Dublin proceeds with unexampled dispatch. They are in general about forty feet in diameter, precisely circular, and built of hewn granite closely jointed. Some are already thirty feet high, and exhibit proofs of the most admirable masonry.'

The twenty-one Martello towers erected between 1804 and 1806 along the coast of Dublin at a cost of £1,800 each, formed part of the large number of these fortifications built by the British to help repel the threat of a French invasion during the Napoleonic Wars.

The name Martello comes from a similar round tower at Cape Mortella on the island of Corsica which was captured by the British navy in 1794. The small, lightly armed garrison of the tower had earlier managed to repel British attacks by land and sea, inflicting sixty casualties and causing great damage to some of their frigates in the process. The British were so impressed with the defensive capabilities of the Mortella tower that they built a string of them across the south coast of England and along the Irish coast.

John Carr, who wrote a memoir of his travels through Ireland in 1805, was scathing in his assessment of the military value of the towers. He wrote: 'I believe it would require the inflamed imagination of the hero of Cervantes [Don Quixote] to discover one possible military advantage which they possess, placed as they are at such a distance, on account of the shallowness of the bay, from the possibility of annoying a hostile vessel.'

The Martello towers were not built to a standard size but the design was roughly the same in each. The outer walls of the towers are approximately ten feet thick. Inside, the towers there was an upper and a lower floor. The upper floor was the living quarters for the garrison and it contained a fireplace for cooking and heating purposes. Ammunition and provisions were stored on the lower floor and a steel tank was sunk into the floor for the storage of drinking water. The roof, which was accessed by a spiral staircase within the tower, contained a gun mounted on a carriage and a shot furnace that was used to manufacture red-hot shot which could be used to set fire to enemy ships. Access to the tower was usually via a doorway located roughly twenty feet off the ground, usually by a ladder that could be pulled up into the tower.

Today we can only speculate as to the effectiveness of the Martello towers as the expected invasion never materialised. For many years afterwards the towers were put to a variety of uses. Some were used as bathing-boxes and seaside dwellings while others saw service as launderettes. Today, many of the towers stand abandoned and silent but others have been given a new lease of life as converted dwelling-houses or as repositories, such as the James Joyce Museum at Sandycove.

The Martello tower at Sandycove is mentioned in the first chapter of James Joyce's *Ulysses* and it now houses exhibits relating to the life of James Joyce. Joyce mentions William Pitt who was responsible for the erection of the towers: 'Billy Pitt had them built, Buck Mulligan said, when the French were on the sea.' The towers have also been referred to as 'Billy Pitt's follies' possibly because of the fact that they cost so much to build and were never used.

Ha'penny Bridge

The Ha'penny Bridge over the River Liffey is one of the most enduring images of the city and is probably one of the most photographed bridges in Ireland. The image of this famous old bridge has adorned millions of postcards over the decades and no book, film or TV programme related to Dublin can be complete without a reference to it.

The place where the bridge was built was once the location of one of the many ferries that traversed the river. The mooring point on the south bank was known as the Bagnio Slip. The name Bagnio is believed to originate from an early eighteenth-century Temple Bar brothel.

The idea for a toll-bridge was conceived in 1815 by John 'Bloody' Beresford – a member of Dublin Corporation – and a man named William Walsh. Walsh approached the Coalbrookdale Ironworks in Shropshire with his scheme to build a single-span metal bridge over the Liffey. The bridge was made in eighteen separate sections and transported to Dublin.

The bridge, which was originally called the Wellington Bridge (although it was never officially named so) in honour of the duke of Wellington's victory at the Battle of Waterloo, was opened to the public without fuss or fanfare on 19 May 1816 and pedestrians were allowed to cross toll-free for the first ten days. From then on a toll of one halfpenny was charged. Beresford had originally erected toll-houses at either end of the bridge but these were removed just a few months later.

The name of Wellington Bridge didn't rest easily with many Dubliners, who remembered some of Beresford's activities during the rebellion of 1798 when he and his 'bloodhounds' had tortured suspected rebels at his home in Marlborough Street. Some referred to the new bridge as the 'Triangle Bridge', a reference to Beresford's use of a triangular scaffold to torture the rebels.

The Wellington Bridge title must not have lasted too long as twenty years later it was being referred to in official documents as the 'Metal Bridge'. It has also in times past been called the Iron Bridge and the Cast-Iron Bridge. Today, the official title of the structure is the Liffey Bridge but no Dubliner in living memory and beyond has ever called it anything but the 'Ha'penny Bridge'.

In 1912 the art dealer and collector Sir Hugh Lane came up with a scheme to replace the bridge with an art gallery and he commissioned Sir Edwin Lutyens to design it for him. Lane proposed that Dublin Corporation would pull down what he referred to as 'the hideous metal bridge and to build a gallery on a stone faced bridge'. In return he promised to fill it with paintings from his own impressive collection. Although Lane's proposal was backed by people such as W.B. Yeats, Dublin Corporation turned down his request on the basis that it would prove too costly.

Over the years there were several campaigns to abolish the toll on the bridge but Dublin Corporation were powerless to do anything about it until the 99-year lease expired. Ownership of the bridge finally reverted into the hands of the corporation in September 1916. The Ha'penny Bridge ceased to be a toll-bridge on 25 March 1919, when the turnstiles were removed and it was thrown open for the free usage of the people of Dublin.

First Hanging

Thursday 7 March 1901 is a notable date in the history of Mountjoy Prison as it marks the first occasion that a prisoner was hanged in the gaol. Dublin man John Toole earned this dubious distinction after his conviction for the murder of his common-law wife.

John Toole, a Dublin cab driver had been separated from his wife and three children for a number of years and in December 1900 he was living in a rented room at 45 Charlemont Street with his new partner Lizzie Brennan. On the night of 1 December, Toole and Brennan returned to Charlemont Street following a heavy drinking session.

The next morning, worried neighbours who had been woken by strange noises in the house tried to gain access to the room but were unable to do so. The police were called and after breaking down the door they discovered the lifeless body of Lizzie Brennan, her throat having been slashed from ear to ear. Beside her lay the sleeping form of John Toole. Toole also had a throat wound but it was only a minor one. He was then taken to the Meath Hospital where he admitted trying to take his own life but denied killing Lizzie Brennan.

Toole was subsequently charged with the murder of

Lizzie Brennan and his trial – presided over by Mr Justice Kenny – began on 7 February 1901. The judge decided that Toole's actions had been premeditated and after only a few minutes of weighing up the evidence the jury returned a guilty verdict.

Donning the black cap, Justice Kenny sentenced Toole to death, telling him that he would be taken to Mountjoy where he would be 'hanged by the neck until you be dead, and that your body be buried within the walls of the prison in which the aforesaid judgement shall be executed upon you, and may God in his mercy, have mercy on your soul.'

Toole's legal team appealed to the Lord Lieutenant for clemency on behalf of the prisoner but it was turned down. Mountjoy's first hanging would take place on 7 March as originally decreed by Justice Kenny.

Toole spent his last night on earth in the condemned cell. On the morning of his execution he refused breakfast and attended mass in the prison chapel at 7 a.m. Just before 8 o'clock he was taken to the scaffold that been erected in the prison's central courtyard. The grim procession to Toole's place of execution included the governor of Mountjoy, Captain MacMurray, the prison chaplain, the prison doctor, the sub-sheriff and six prison officers.

On reaching the execution chamber, Toole was placed on the trapdoor of the gallows, his feet were bound together and a white linen hood was placed over his head. The travelling hangman, T.H. Scott, who had come over from England to carry out the execution, placed the noose around the condemned man's neck and at precisely 8 o'clock he pulled the lever, launching Toole into eternity.

Outside the prison the large crowd that had gathered on the North Circular Road to witness the event were informed of Toole's death by the raising of a black flag high over the prison. The prisoner's body was later taken down from the scaffold and buried in the prison graveyard.

Custom House Fire

'Awful Fire at the Custom-House Stores' was the dramatic headline that appeared in *Saunders Newsletter* on 10 August 1833.

This was as near a live report as you were going to get in Dublin 170 years ago as the newspaper gave an hour-by-hour report of a devastating fire that took place at the city's Custom House during the early hours of 10 August.

The blaze was described in the *Freeman's Journal* as the 'greatest fire which ever took place in Dublin' and 'was seen with a brilliancy little diminished at Kingstown, and illuminated the firmament with light resembling day for miles around the city'.

Large crowds flocked from all parts of Dublin to witness the spectacle and the flames could be seen for miles around. Even ships thirty miles out in the Irish Sea reported seeing the blaze.

The Custom House itself was lit up as if it was midday rather than the middle of the night and the blaze could be seen from all parts of the city. Hundreds of kegs of whiskey were thrown into the Liffey to stop them from exploding and the quays and surrounding streets were ablaze with rivers of whiskey pouring from hundreds of damaged spirit kegs. Some of this burning whiskey flowed into the Liffey and ignited the barrels that had been thrown in earlier and the river was described as 'a sheet of flame for half of its breadth.'

However, it wasn't all bad news. One newspaper reported that several bystanders and night watchmen managed to salvage a bucket of whiskey from the blazing building and were said to have been drinking it by the mugful. Sailors who had gathered on Custom House Quay to view the spectacle were reported to be 'beastly drunk'.

The fire, believed to be accidental, broke out at around 2 a.m. on Saturday morning at the sugar and wine stores at the Custom House on the North Wall. The blaze quickly took hold and stores of spirits, oil and tallow further fuelled the flames. Fire engines and water carts converged on the scene from all over the city but they were useless against the severity of the inferno.

The blaze was eventually subdued and the labourers and dock workers who turned out to man the pumps on that night won great praise for their unstinting efforts. Working throughout the night and 'refreshed at intervals with porter', the men, with a little help from the weather, managed to confine the blaze to the sugar and wine stores. One fireman was horribly maimed when he fell into what was described as 'a boiling mass of molten sugar', while another was so overcome by whiskey fumes that he became violent and had to be restrained. He eventually threw himself into the river and was only rescued with a great deal of difficulty.

For a few hours, it seemed as if the flames would consume the Custom House itself but a timely change in wind direction prevented this from happening. Nonetheless, the fire continued to burn for another three days until it was eventually subdued.

Many Dublin merchants suffered substantial losses in the blaze. In the aftermath of the disaster it was estimated that 700 puncheons (large barrels) of whiskey were destroyed along with 5,000 casks of sugar. Large quantities of champagne, claret and burgundy and a range of other goods such as tallow, oil, hemp, silk and even a consignment of pianos were lost.

The traders were compensated to the tune of £68,000 some months later when a petition, presented to the British Government on their behalf by Daniel O'Connell, was successful.

Frank Du Bedat

Financial scandals in Dublin aren't just a twenty-first-century phenomenon as evidenced by the case that came before the courts in 1891. One year earlier Frank Du Bedat, who was a member of a well-established Dublin banking family, took his place as the head of William George Du Bedat & Sons, Government Stock and Share Brokers at Foster Place next door to the Bank of Ireland in College Green.

This well-respected old Dublin Huguenot family's motto 'Sans Tache' translates as 'Without Stain' but within a very short space of time, due to Frank Du Bedat's activities, the firm's reputation for honesty was in tatters.

Frank – a large man weighing over twenty stone – had a flamboyant lifestyle and expensive tastes. To his friends, he was known as 'the Baron' and on his many trips to Europe he spent money freely. He also bought Stoneleigh, a large mansion in Killiney, and began to spend large amounts of money on an extensive renovation project. In order to fund his extravagant lifestyle, Du Bedat began to gamble on the Stock Exchange using money taken from his clients' accounts.

At the pinnacle of his career, when he had just turned forty, Du Bedat was elected President of the Dublin Stock Exchange in October 1890. This was to prove a very short-lived appointment, however, as within weeks he was ruined.

Du Bedat realised that he could never make up his losses and he fled Dublin on Christmas Eve of that year, leaving a note for his wife Rosa and debts totalling over £100,000.

Six months later Du Bedat was arrested in Capetown in South Africa and was brought back to Dublin to face charges of bankruptcy and fraud. On 20 October 1891, one year after his election as President of the Dublin Stock Exchange, Du Bedat went on trial at Green Street courthouse for his crimes. He was found guilty as charged and he received a seven-year sentence with twelve months hard labour.

Sentencing him Justice Holmes said:

Francis Du Bedat ... when you entered upon life you were endowed by those who bore your name with a rich inheritance in the reputation for honour and honesty ... you took another course, you chose to make a rush for riches and the race for greed as so often happens has ended in ruin to yourself, bitter memories to others and benefit to none.

Du Bedat was sent to Mountjoy where he suffered from ill health due to a ruptured hernia which he sustained during his trial after falling from a cab. He lost ten stone during his incarceration and in 1896 he was transferred to Maryborough Prison (Portlaoise) and released soon afterwards.

The following year Frank travelled to South Africa where he tried to re-establish himself as a financial guru. He returned to Dublin a few years later with a South American actress in tow and they lived in Malahide for a time.

Du Bedat was arrested for fraud again in 1903 following a disastrous Portuguese venture and he was sentenced to four years' penal servitude. He was sent to serve his sentence at Maryborough but he was released by the lord lieutenant having served only a few weeks of his sentence when new evidence cast doubt on his conviction.

Du Bedat returned to South Africa with his new wife Rosita and hoped to begin a new life. They lived in a village called Kommetjie on the Cape Peninsula.

Frank Du Bedat died penniless on 20 July 1919 at the age of seventy years.

St Stephen's Green

St Stephen's Green has been one of Dublin's most fashionable areas since the city's gentry built their homes there in the eighteenth century. The lands were originally part of the thirteenth century St Stephen's Leper Hospital. Mercer's Hospital was later built on this site and for almost 400 years the green was common pasture used by the citizens of Dublin for the grazing of cattle and sheep.

Some attempts were made to clean up the area during the seventeenth century, but it didn't really begin to develop until 1815, when the common was fenced in. Prior to this a badly kept hedge and a large ditch, which was apparently used as a repository for the city's refuse, had surrounded the green.

In 1815 twenty acres were reserved for a park and eighty-nine plots of land surrounding the green were sold off to various developers. Within a short time the green was surrounded by the fashionable dwellings that we now know so well.

From 1815 until 1880 the green was reserved for the exclusive use of the residents of the area who had their own keys to the park. But the park was opened to the public in 1880 after Lord Ardilaun of the Guinness family paid £20,000 to have it laid out in its present form.

The four sides of the green had different names. The north side was called the Beaux Walk and became a fashionable meeting place. The south was called Leeson's Walk after Joseph Leeson who lived there. The east side of the park was known as the 'Monks Walk', while the west side was known as the French Walk, so called because of the number of French Huguenots living in the area.

Over the years the green was used for many purposes. The citizens marched to the green every May Day and the Freemen of Dublin marched in military formation past the mayor and aldermen, who had gathered in a marquee specially erected for the occasion.

The green was also used for football and other sporting activities, which sometimes got out of hand and turned into major riots.

For many years Stephen's Green was a place of execution and on Saturday 21 August 1784 thousands gathered there to witness the execution of Mary Fairfield, who was sentenced to death for the murder of a wet nurse named Mary Funt. Fairfield was taken to the green from her cell at Newgate prison in a cart. There she was strangled by the hangman who then flung her lifeless body into a fire.

The last hanging to take place at St Stephen's Green was that of Patrick Dougherty who was executed there on 21 December 1782. Dougherty was sentenced to death for the armed robbery of an Ormond Quay wine merchant, Thomas Moran. Moran testified against Dougherty in court and he was hanged three days later. After Dougherty's body was cut down from the gallows his family and friends seized the corpse and brought it to the door of Moran's house at Ormond Quay. The Dublin Volunteers then snatched the body back and attempted to bring it to the anatomists at Trinity College for dissection. On reaching Trinity, the Volunteers – with Dougherty's family and friends in hot pursuit – found the gates of the college locked against them.

The Volunteers were forced to hand over Dougherty's body which was then taken away to be buried at an unknown location. Soon afterwards the lord lieutenant took steps to ensure that there would be no repeat of these bizarre scenes and he ordered that all future hangings would take place at the front of Newgate prison in Green Street.

White Quakers

Joshua Jacob, a member of the Dublin biscuit-making family, was born at Clonmel in 1802. He was educated in England and at the famous Quaker School at Ballitore in Kildare. Afterwards, he came to Dublin where he found employment at Cavert's the Candlemakers in Thomas Street. He married for the first time in 1829 and established a business at the 'Sign of the Teapot' in Nicholas Street where he ran a tea shop and grocer's store.

Joshua was an active member of the Dublin Quakers, or the Society of Friends as they were known, but he believed that too many of his contemporaries were destroying the society in their quest for wealth.

Joshua and about thirty other members of the community decided that a more severe brand of Quakerism was required and they broke away to form a group that came to be known as the 'White Quakers'. The new group, who dedicated themselves to a simple and frugal lifestyle, were so called because they only wore white clothing and painted all of their furniture white. Joshua also decided that all symbols of pride and ostentation were surplus to the new group's requirements and he smashed all of the mirrors in his house at Nicholas Street. He developed a particular distaste for bells, watches and clocks, believing them to be the work of the devil and he was once thrown out of a friend's house for setting fire to a bell rope there.

The group's first headquarters in Dublin was at 64 William Street, where they stayed from 1840 until 1843, when they were evicted following a court case. They then moved to large premises on Usshers Quay that had formerly been Holmes Hotel. P.J. McCall in his *Shadow of St Patrick's* makes an intriguing reference to the White Quakers' 'nude procession' to the hotel, calling it 'one of the strangest sights of this century in Dublin'.

In keeping with his extreme beliefs Jacob liquidated all of his assets and donated the proceeds to the common fund of the White Quakers. Joshua's brother had died some time previously leaving a widow and six children and Joshua gave their trust fund to the White Quakers.

The executors of the will took legal action against Joshua and he was sent to the Four Courts Marshalsea prison off Thomas Street. He had two rooms in the Marshalsea and he spent three and a half years there writing pamphlets and newspaper articles in support of the White Quakers. He was even allowed to hold the occasional prayer meeting in the prison yard during his stay there. He was eventually released due to ill health in 1846.

On his release Joshua went to live at the community's new home at Newlands in Clondalkin. By 1851, Jacob and the White Quakers had moved to a house known as 'The Sabine Fields' at Scholarstown near Rathfarnham. He seems to have given up his interest in Quakerism at this time after his second marriage, to Catherine Devine, a young Cork widow. The couple's children were subsequently baptised in the Catholic church in Celbridge and the former 'Apostle of the White Quakers' himself was baptised as a Catholic there in 1859.

Joshua Jacob died at the home of his son John in Clondalkin in 1877 at the age of seventy-six. He was buried at Glasnevin, not with his former companions in the White Quaker plot in the southern section of the cemetery, but in a separate family grave with his wife Catherine and one of their sons.

Prince of Pickpockets

One of the best-known thieves of late eighteenth century Dublin and London was George Barrington who was also known as 'The Prince of Pickpockets' or the 'Arch Pickpocket'.

Barrington, alias Waldron, was born in Maynooth in 1755, the son of a local silversmith. Although his parents were poor, they managed to provide young George with a decent education, most of which he received in Dublin.

However, his schooling ended abruptly at the age of sixteen in 1771 when he got into a quarrel with one of his classmates and stabbed him with a pen-knife. Barrington fled from Dublin to Drogheda, where he teamed up with a travelling theatre company owned by a convicted London fraudster, John Price.

Price had been sentenced to be transported to America for his crimes, but had escaped and fled to Ireland. Barrington had a natural talent for acting and for a time he enjoyed a reasonable amount of success on the stage. His biographer said that he 'had a speaking eye, an expressive countenance, a tolerable theatrical figure, a very pompous enunciation, and a most retentive memory'.

The theatre company fell on hard times and Barrington decided that the life of a gentleman thief was infinitely more rewarding than that of an actor and he soon rose to the very top of his new profession.

Barrington initially preyed on members of London's high society and no pocket or purse was safe from 'the prince of pickpockets'. On one particular occasion he gate-crashed the Queen of England's birthday party dressed as a parson and managed to pick several pockets without being detected. On another occasion he was thrown out of the House of Lords when he was spotted by a member of the house while going about his business.

Following several stints in prison Barrington decided that London was getting too hot for him and decided to try his hand in Dublin and he made several visits to the city during his criminal career. He sometimes visited Dublin in the company of the bare-knuckle boxer Daniel Mendoza and a team of his criminal cronies, using the fighter's bouts as cover for their criminal activities.

The *Freeman's Journal* announced Barrington's return to Dublin in February of 1788 in much the same fashion as a visit from a famous actor or other performer:

> By various accounts, the noted and famous Barrington is lately arrived in this city: doubtless he intends honouring some of our crowded churches, the law courts, Promenade, Theatre, and other public places, to keep in practice his unrivalled sleight of hand.

One of Barrington's most infamous and daring robberies took place in March 1790 when it was reported that he picked the pockets of thirty wealthy members of the congregation attending a charity sermon at St Mary's Church in Mary Street. The *Dublin Morning Post* also reported that Lady Charlemont was taken for the princely sum of twenty guineas by the 'prince of pickpockets'.

Despite the widespread reporting of Barrington's alleged Dublin crimes, he was never actually caught in the act. However, during his extended crime spree in London he was arrested and imprisoned on at least seventeen separate occasions.

Barrington's life of crime finally came to an end when he was sentenced to seven years' transportation to Australia in 1791. On arrival at Botany Bay he was rewarded for his good behaviour on the voyage with the post of Superintendent of Convicts at Parramatta in Sydney's western suburbs. Later on he turned the full circle from poacher to gamekeeper when he became chief constable of Parramatta, which his biographer in the *Newgate Calendar* claimed: 'testified the sincerity of his reformation, and rendered him a useful member of society for the remainder of his life.'

Church Street Disaster

On 2 September 1913, two four-storey tenement houses in Church Street collapsed killing seven people and injuring many more, and eleven families were left homeless.

A DMP man, Sergeant Long, who had been walking the beat on Arran Quay, heard the crash of the falling buildings and immediately made his way to the scene of the disaster.

On arrival at Church Street he found that numbers 66 and 67 directly opposite the Father Matthew Temperance Hall had collapsed.

Long immediately called the fire brigade and began the grim task of searching the rubble for survivors with a number of other DMP men and civilian volunteers.

A report in the *Evening Herald* of 3 September described the grim scene:

> ... the first body come upon was that of a woman, Mrs. Fagan. A few yards away a little boy lying in his little cot slept the sleep of death ... the little fellow who had long golden hair and was aged about five, must have been alive up to about three o'clock this morning. There was a look of fear

and anguish on his tear stained face, and he had grasped the sheet convulsively in his death agony.' It emerged afterwards that this was the body of three-year-old John Shiels.

Towards dawn, rescuers heard a dog barking in the rubble. Soon afterwards they discovered the frightened animal lying trapped under a fallen beam, next to the body of a man who had perished in the disaster. A slightly injured black cat was also found near by.

In all, fifteen tenants were removed from the rubble with eight surviving. The dead were named as: Peter Crowley (6), Elizabeth Fagan (50), Nicholas Fitzpatrick (40), Margaret Rourke (56), Elizabeth Salmon (4), Eugene Salmon (17) and John Shiels (3).

The owner of the tenements, Mrs. Margaret Ryan, who lived in a house at the rear of the premises, said afterwards that she had been talking to one of her tenants, Teresa Timmins, in 67 when they heard a loud noise coming from number 66. The women ran next door where they found some of the tenants looking at a marble mantelpiece that had fallen in one of the front rooms of the house. Margaret Ryan said afterwards that she heard a series of sharp cracks followed by a rumbling sound. The women, including the landlady, attempted to flee the building at that stage. Mrs Ryan and some of the others managed to escape, but fifteen tenants were trapped in the building.

The true cause of the collapse was never established but it emerged afterwards that the houses had been inspected two months earlier by an inspector of dangerous buildings from Dublin Corporation. The inspector, a Mr Derham, had issued the landlady with an order to erect a beam across the top of one of the houses and to repair a pier between the two buildings. Mrs. Ryan had the necessary work carried out immediately and the building was passed as being safe for habitation by the corporation.

Commenting on the tragedy shortly afterwards, the lord mayor of Dublin, Alderman Coffey, said that while he didn't want to apportion blame for the tragedy, a great deal of responsibility lay with the Local Government Board for having delayed giving the go ahead for a scheme to replace the old tenements with new houses. He was also of the opinion that 'heavy lorries like Guinness' speeding up and down the city's quays were having a detrimental effect on 'old and shaky' tenements in the city.

Jonathan Swift

Jonathan Swift was born on 30 November 1667 at a house on Hoey's Court adjoining Werburgh Street. Swift's father, also called Jonathan, died some months before the birth of his son leaving Swift's mother destitute and dependent on the generosity of her husband's family.

While still a babe in arms, Swift was taken – some say kidnapped – by his nurse and brought to her home town of Whitehaven in Cumberland. By the time he returned to Dublin at the age of three, Swift's mother had departed for her family home in Leicester leaving the young Swift in the care of his father's brother Godwin. (Swift's Alley near Francis Street was apparently named after this member of the Swift family).

The young Swift was despatched to Kilkenny for his schooling and he entered Trinity College in 1682 at the age of fifteen. Swift didn't appear to have been too concerned with his studies as he only received his degree 'by special grace' which basically means that he had 'pull'. During his time at Trinity, Swift was often in trouble with the college authorities for his poor attendance record, unruly behaviour and fighting and he was once censured for 'neglect of duties and frequenting of the town'.

Despite his troubles, Swift remained at Trinity for another three years while studying for an advanced degree. At the outbreak of the Williamite wars in 1689, Swift left Ireland for England where he worked as a secretary to Sir William Temple at Moor Park in Surrey. He returned to Ireland to become a Church of Ireland minister in 1694 and was ordained at Christ Church the following year.

Having served his time in a number of parishes throughout Ireland, Swift became dean of St Patrick's Cathedral in Dublin, a position that he held until his death in 1745.

Swift is chiefly remembered for his writing, and his best-known work, *Gulliver's Travels*, was published in 1726. Most of his writings were political and religious satires, such as *Tale of a Tub* and *The Battle of the Books* published in 1704. He began to take an interest in the politics of Ireland and he became increasingly concerned about the scenes of dire poverty and distress that he witnessed on a daily basis on his travels throughout the city.

In 1720 Swift published his pamphlet *A Proposal for the Universal Use of Irish Manufacture* in which he urged Dubliners to boycott English made goods. Four years later in his famous *Drapier's Letters* Swift thwarted an attempt by the British Government to saturate Ireland with an inferior copper currency known as 'Wood's Halfpence'.

By 1728 Swift's health began to deteriorate. He suffered enormously from Meniere's disease, a condition that causes nausea, deafness and vertigo. The disease was not treatable in Swift's day and he gradually lost the power of speech. In 1742, three years before his death, Swift lapsed into a coma from which he never recovered and he died on 19 October 1745.

As news of Swift's death spread in 1745, large crowds of Dubliners flocked to his house to pay their last respects. According to Thomas Sheridan – Swift's godson – many in the crowd managed to obtain locks of Swifts hair by bribing his servants. 'In less than an hour' said Sheridan, 'his venerable head was entirely stripped of all its silver ornaments, so that not a hair remained.'

Swift's remains lie in St Patrick's Cathedral where, as the inscription beside his tomb reads: ' ... fierce indignation can no more lacerate his heart. Go traveller, and imitate, if you can, one who strove with all his strength to champion liberty.'

Rochdale Disaster

On the night of Wednesday 18 November 1807, two of the worst shipping disasters ever to befall the city took place off Dun Laoghaire within hours of each other, leading to a total loss of almost 400 lives.

Earlier that afternoon, two transport ships – the *Rochdale* and *Prince of Wales* – had set out from the Pigeon House harbour on the Great South Wall. The *Prince of Wales* with 120 soldiers on board was bound for Liverpool, when a violent easterly gale accompanied by driving snow blew up in Dublin Bay. The blizzard, which lasted for nearly two days, was one of the worst ever seen in Dublin as evidenced by a report in the *Freeman's Journal* a week later:

> So great a fall of snow, at so early a period of the season, and in so short a time as that which fell on Thursday and Friday last in the vicinity of the metropolis, and, we believe, generally throughout Ireland, has not been remembered by the oldest person living.

On Thursday morning the *Prince of Wales* was spotted just outside Dublin Bay and it was believed that the crew were trying to return to the harbour. However, with visibility almost nil and the storm still raging, the hapless ship was driven onto the rocks at Blackrock. The captain launched the ship's long boat immediately and made for the shore. Only seventeen people – including the captain, ship steward's wife and child – made it into the boat. The remaining 120 passengers left behind

– mainly British soldiers – all perished and most of them were buried in Merrion cemetery on the Merrion Road.

Following an inquest into the disaster, the master of the ship, Robert Jones, along with the mate and steward, were charged with the murder of the passengers, and it was alleged that they had removed ladders from the hold in order to get away in the long boat themselves. The trial, which was due to be heard in December, was abandoned due to lack of evidence.

The *Rochdale*, which left Dublin on the same day with 265 passengers on board as well as the crew, met a similar fate, leading to an even greater loss of life. Like the *Prince of Wales*, the *Rochdale* was observed in a distressed condition off Blackrock on Thursday. The crew made frantic attempts to signal for help but due to the atrocious weather conditions no assistance was forthcoming. The ship ran aground on rocks close to the Martello tower at Seapoint, not far from the site of the earlier tragedy. It was remarkable that despite the fact that the ship ran aground so close to the shore, not one person managed to reach land alive.

The bodies of the dead from both disasters were washed up along the coast from Blackrock to Bullock harbour and the *Freeman's Journal* of 24 November reported a 'scene of horror … shocking beyond description' with countless 'mangled and mutilated bodies of both sexes' strewn along a two-mile stretch of coastline while the bodies of several women were washed up with the corpses of their infant children still clutched in their arms.

Two smaller ships also went down in Dublin Bay during the storm but received little attention in the Dublin newspapers. A collier sank somewhere off Kingstown (Dun Laoghaire) with the loss of all hands while a trading vessel belonging to Robert Shaw was also lost, and again there were no survivors.

Ball-bearing

During the Middle Ages, the annual festivals of Corpus Christi and, to a lesser extent, St George's Day, were the highlights of the social calendar in Dublin. No expense was spared for the pageants, and thousands turned out to see the city's guilds led by the mayor of Dublin, march through the streets of the city in the most colourful events of the year.

Each year, the guilds were commanded by the mayor and bailiffs of the city on the basis of 'an olde lawe' to assemble on these feast days to enact religious plays and pageants assigned to them by the mayor. These annual events were lavish productions and were a source of great pride for the guilds and Dubliners in general.

From the year 1512 onwards the mayor of Dublin was forced to walk barefoot at the head of the Corpus Christi procession in atonement for an attack by some of the citizens of Dublin in which St Patrick's Cathedral was desecrated and ransacked, in what was described as a: '… heathenish riot of the citizens of Dublin rushing into the church armed, polluting with slaughter the consecrated place, defacing the images, prostrating the relics, razing down the altars with barbarous outcries …'

One of the most curious annual civic events to take place in the city during those years was the Shrovetide 'bearing of balls' procession enacted by young, newly married Dublin males.

Today many men and women would claim that marriage is a cross to be borne, but in the Dublin of the fifteenth century, newly wed Dublin men were forced to carry small decorated balls through the streets of the city in an annual ritual that occurred every Shrove Tuesday.

This little mentioned practice was sometimes referred to as 'Corperaunt Day' and was first mentioned in a Dublin context in 1462. Young men who had wed during the previous year were expected to take part in the procession and to pay a levy to the corporation.

The various guilds of Dublin took part in the pageant, marching in a strict pre-ordained sequence as on other occasions such as Corpus Christi and St George's day. In an article written on this topic in 1925, Myles Ronan states that the bearing of balls was a tradition that originated at Chester in England, where decorated balls were awarded as prizes in racing and archery competitions. These balls were afterwards exchanged for bells. Other writers have disputed Ronan's assertion, claiming that the evidence for the Chester tradition is much later than that of Dublin.

The practice of ball bearing in Dublin was first mentioned in Dublin Corporation Assembly records for 1462 when it was decreed that 'all manner of men of the said city, as well as clerks of court as other men (being wedded) shall bear their ball upon this day upon the pain of ten shillings, half thereof to be paid to the Mayor for the time being and the other half to the treasuries of the said city'. It was apparently quite a serious offence to ignore this edict as defaulters were liable to be arrested by the bailiffs and imprisoned until the fine was paid.

One of the last known references to the practice is seen in the Dublin Assembly Rolls of 21 January 1569 when the mayor issued the following instructions for the procession: 'It is agreed for eschewing controversy that may arise on Shrove Tuesday in bearing balls that every occupation to keep order in riding with their balls as they are appointed to go with their pageants on Corpus Christi day.'

May Day

In olden times the ancient feast of Bealtaine was celebrated in Ireland to welcome in the new summer season. In more recent times, the May Day ceremonies played a big part in the social calendar of the Irish people, and in many parts of Dublin it was one of the most eagerly anticipated events of the whole year.

The biggest May Day celebrations in the city took place in the Liberties and the largest bonfire in the city was lit on an open space near St Patrick's Cathedral along with many other fires in the back lanes and alleyways of the Liberties. The weavers had their own bonfire at Weaver's Square while the hatters held their celebrations at James' Street. There was another bonfire at St John's Well near Kilmainham while the major celebration on the north bank of the Liffey took place at Smithfield.

Every year, during the days and weeks leading up to May Day, 'May-boys' toured the city collecting money and whiskey for the festivities. Some of the money was spent on turf and logs for the bonfire and old tar barrels to keep the blaze going throughout the night. Curiously, many of the bonfires contained a blazing horse's skull which took pride of place perched on top of the fire. The significance of having a blazing horse's skull on the fire isn't clear but they and other animal bones were donated from local knackers' yards and tanners yards at Kilmainham.

An unnamed scribe writing in 1825 commented that the practice of dragging these bones to the fires led to a term of abuse that was in common usage in Dublin during that era: so if someone told you that they were going to 'drag you like a horse's head to a bonfire' it didn't mean that they wanted to take you for a pint!

During the lead-up to May Day, rioting between the various Dublin gangs was commonplace as one would try to snatch the other's May-bush, which was central to the celebrations.

There was fierce competition between the warring factions as to which area could display the finest May-bush and they often went to great lengths to secure a suitable one. The bush, usually a thorn bush, was selected well in advance of May-day and on the day before the festival a large crowd, armed with axes, saws and ropes descended on the chosen tree to cut it down and carry it home for the revels later on.

These excursions sometimes led to serious disturbances that had to be broken up by the police as the May-boys sometimes chose thorn bushes that had been growing in a private garden or lawn, much to the irritation of the owner.

The May-bush was decorated with lighted candles, ribbons and baubles in very much the same fashion as a Christmas tree is today and it took pride of place beside the bonfire before it was thrown into the fire at the end of the night.

In many rural parts of North County Dublin and Fingal it was part of the May Day tradition for gangs of young men and women to roam through their areas carrying emblems that represented their various trades.

Each May Day morning or on the following Sunday, known as 'Sonnoughing Sunday', they would set out from their homes; the women carried peeled hazel rods, or white wands, while the men carried a symbol that represented their trade. Labourers bore spades, sweeps carried their brushes, threshers flourished flails, while cowherds would carry a hazel rod which had had its tip blackened in the May Day bonfire for luck.

City Guilds

During the Middle Ages, the trade and religious guilds of Dublin were very much part of the social and commercial fabric of the city and they could be very loosely described as being the forerunners of modern-day trade unions. The guilds fall into two categories: social-religious guilds and trade guilds, which were divided into merchant guilds and guilds organised on a craft basis.

Myles Ronan's general description of what the Dublin trade guilds were about, in an article written for the *Irish Ecclesiastical Record* written during the 1930s is as good as any: 'They were essentially lay bodies, composed of women as well as men; assistance to brethren in poverty or distress, the settlement of quarrels without litigation, and the regulation of their trade or business, to the exclusion of all "intruders" were among their first principles.'

The first guilds were known in Italy and France as far back as the eighth century while they were common in Denmark, England, Norway and the Netherlands during the eleventh century. From the twelfth century onwards the guild was an important feature of the economic and social life of most European countries.

There were three different grades of membership of the guild. The master, who was elected by the membership on an annual basis, the journeymen and apprentices. A journeyman was someone who had served his time as an apprentice. Apprentices were bound to their masters for a fixed term of years. During the early years of the guild system this term was at the discretion of the master. However, some masters abused this system and the term of apprenticeship was later fixed to seven years.

There were approximately twenty-five guilds in Dublin at various stages with the Merchant's Guild, also called the Guild of the Holy Trinity, being the most powerful. This Merchant's Guild held a virtual monopoly on all trading activity within the city until the end of the seventeenth century.

The Tailor's Hall in Back Lane behind High Street is Dublin's only surviving guild hall. The Tailor's Guild was formed in 1420. The original Tailor's Hall was situated in Winetavern Street and was first mentioned in 1538. The new Tailor's Hall was built in 1708 and several other guilds such as the barber-surgeons, brewers, butchers and shoemakers held their meetings there.

The Guild of the Blessed Virgin Mary, commonly known as the Weaver's Guild, dates from as far back as the twelfth century and was at one time one of the biggest and most influential of Dublin's guilds.

Other guilds in the city included the Goldsmith's Guild, the Guild of Carpenters, Millers, Masons and Heliers (Slaters), the Cook's and Vintner's Guild, and the Guild of Tallow Chandlers, Soap boilers and Wax-light Makers. Royal charter established the Guild of Barber-Surgeons and Apothecaries in 1446.

Some other trades represented by guilds were: clockmakers, watchmakers, coopers, glovers and skinners, felt-makers, blacksmiths, bricklayers, plasterers, curriers, painters, butchers, and the brewers and maltsters.

The guild system lasted until 1840 when an act of Parliament allowed for the public election of members of Dublin Corporation for the first time. The act broke centuries of tradition whereby the guilds of the city had an automatic entitlement to hold a number of seats on the corporation.

Wellington

Arthur Wellesley, commander of the British forces at the Battle of Waterloo, otherwise known as the duke of Wellington or 'Iron Duke', was born at 24 Upper Merrion Street in Dublin on 1 May 1769. The Wellington Monument in the Phoenix Park, built to commemorate Wellesley's military triumphs, stands at 205 feet tall and is one of the tallest obelisks in the world.

On 20 July 1813, *Faulkner's Dublin Journal* gave details of a meeting to be held later that evening at the Rotunda rooms to discuss the erection of a 'Monument to Lord Wellington' in order to express what the newspaper described as 'a nation's admiration of the transcendent exploits of her son and hero' in Spain, Portugal and France.

A year later, with subscriptions amounting to nearly £16,000 in the bank, a committee was established to decide on a suitable monument to honour Wellington and to select an appropriate location to house it. The committee, which consisted of eighty-five people, then held a competition to select the monument and they received a large number of entries. The top six models, which included two obelisks, three columns and a temple, were then put on display at the Royal Dublin Society's premises at Hawkins Street and the obelisk designed by Robert Smirke was chosen.

The committee's next task was to choose a location for the monument and Stephen's Green, Temple Bar, the Royal Barracks (Collins Barracks), Merrion Square, the Rotunda

Gardens and Mountjoy Square along with its present location were all considered.

The lord lieutenant laid the foundation stone for the monument on 17 June 1817 and the obelisk was completed – sixteen feet short of its original target – in 1820. The committee had run out of money at that stage and no one seemed to be willing to advance them any more cash to finish the project.

Following Wellington's death in 1852, fresh efforts were made to have the monument completed and in 1856 three sculptors, Joseph Robinson Kirk, Terence Farrell and John Hogan, were selected to design the three panels on the monument depicting Wellington's victories in the Peninsular and Indian campaigns and also his role in the granting of Catholic emancipation.

Kirk designed the panel depicting Wellington's victory at Seringapatam while Farrell was responsible for the Battle of Waterloo panel. John Hogan was chosen to design the panel representing Wellington's contribution to Catholic emancipation but he died just before it was completed. The panel was completed in Rome by Hogan's son, John Valentine, and the famous Italian sculptor Benzoni. This panel depicts Wellington being crowned with a laurel wreath by Britannia while he hands a scroll of freedom to a figure representing Hibernia. On either side of the duke there are sixteen members of the Houses of Commons who had also voted for emancipation.

When a copy of the completed panel was sent back to Dublin for final approval, William Wilde (father of Oscar) and Charles Bianconi, who were the executors of the elder

Hogan's will, complained that there were too many mistakes in the design. Daniel O'Connell had been depicted without his wig and Bianconi insisted that the 'Liberator' wouldn't be recognised by the public without it, while Hibernia's wolfhound was depicted as an Italian greyhound! Hogan and Benzoni took the criticism on board and the mistakes and a few other minor errors were soon put right.

The Wellington Monument was eventually finished in 1861 and on 18 June of that year, forty-eight years after its original inception in the Rotunda rooms, the obelisk with its new panels was finally opened to public view.

Daly's Coffee House

Throughout the eighteenth and nineteenth centuries, Dame Street was home to a thriving newspaper and book publishing trade. Not surprisingly Dame Street was also well supplied with taverns and 'groggeries' such as the Half Moon Alehouse and the Robin Hood and Still, which was famous for its whiskey. However, all of these establishments paled in comparison with Patrick Daly's coffee house, at 2-3 Dame Street. Daly's was one of the best-known clubs in Ireland at the time and it was mainly frequented by members of the upper classes. It was particularly noted as a gambling joint and it was said that half the landed estates in Ireland had changed hands there during its time.

The club was also one of the watering-holes favoured by the bucks and rakes of the city and it wouldn't have been unusual to see some of the patrons being thrown through the windows. Duelling with pistol and sword was a commonplace occurrence at the club and there were even tales of club members using the statue of St Andrew in St Andrew's Church for target practice!

Daly's moved to a new clubhouse in Foster Place right beside the parliament house building on College Green on 16 February 1791. The new club was, according to John Gilbert, 'furnished in a superb manner, with grand lustres, inlaid tables and marble chimney-pieces; the chairs and sofas were white and gold, covered with the richest Aurora Silk'.

For the convenience of the MP, a special footpath was constructed which led from Parliament House directly to Daly's. As well as being a favourite resort of the MPs, Daly's was popular with members of the Hell-Fire Club and other similar clubs whose sole aim was the pursuit of pleasure.

When Daly died at his other establishment, The Curragh Club in Kildare, the Dublin operation was continued by Peter Depoe, who ran it until 1823 when it was finally closed.

There is a very dubious old tale, which connects Daly's Coffee House with the coining of the modern-day word 'quiz'. The story goes that a drunken member once accepted a bet that he could invent a new word that would become commonplace in the English language. The member is said to have left Daly's during the early hours of Sunday morning and spent the rest of the night travelling around the city and chalking the word 'Quiz' in large letters on the doors of all the main churches.

The next morning, mass-goers from all over the city were said to have been 'burning with curiosity' to know what the word meant. The tale has been dismissed as fictional by several 'experts' but none have been able to come up with a convincing alternative.

Another famous coffee house of a slightly earlier vintage was Lucas' Coffee House at Cork Hill, which was in use at the beginning of the eighteenth century. Just like Daly's, Lucas' Coffee House was very popular with the rich and young rakes of the day. One of these was Talbot Edgeworth, a young eccentric who spent his time and money on duelling and fashionable clothing. Edgeworth, who was related to the author Maria Edgeworth, spent his days in Lucas' parading his finery and challenging strangers to fight him. Edgeworth eventually had a nervous breakdown and died later in a Dublin prison having been disowned by his family.

Lucas' continued in use until 1768 when it, along with several adjoining buildings, was demolished to improve access to Dublin Castle.

Dublin Exhibition

Following the success of the Cork International Exhibition of 1902-1903, the editor of the *Daily Independent*, William T. Dennehy, came up with the idea of holding a similar event in Dublin in order to promote the city's commercial and industrial interests.

A committee was formed to this end at a meeting held in the Shelbourne Hotel on 4 February 1903 and a fund of £150,000 was raised over the following months. The committee had originally inspected three possible sites for the exhibition in the Phoenix Park but eventually decided to hold it on an area of waste ground at Ballsbridge belonging to the earl of Pembroke. The site, which is now Herbert Park, contained fifty-two acres and it was given to Pembroke Urban District Council by the earl to celebrate his son, Lord Herbert's birthday.

The Irish International Exhibition began on 4 May 1907 and it ran until 9 November of that year. During that period, nearly three million visitors passed through its turnstiles. The buildings, housing over 1,000 exhibitions, were elaborate-looking structures constructed from steel frames covered over with plywood and plasterboard and painted white.

The most impressive of these buildings was the Grand Central Palace with its 150-foot-high dome. This giant structure covered nearly three acres of Herbert Park and took 300 tons of steel, 70 tons of galvanized iron and a huge amount of plate glass to construct.

Other major buildings on the site were: the Gallery of Fine Arts, Palace of Industries, Great Palace of the Mechanical Arts, Concert Hall and several restaurants. The exhibition also housed many attractions and amusements including a helter-skelter, water chute, crystal maze, rifle range, an ants' and bees' display, rivers of Ireland and Indian jugglers.

One of the most popular exhibits was the authentic Somali Village, which contained – along with spear-wielding Somali tribesmen – huts, a Somali schoolroom, sheep and goats. A legendary Dublin character – 'The Bird Flanagan' – created uproar at the exhibition when he attempted to kidnap a member of the tribe for a bet!

Another popular exhibit was the giant Battle of Waterloo model that formed part of a Napoleonic art exhibition. The model, which measured 1,250 yards by 520 yards, was built during the 1840s and was said to have closely represented conditions at Waterloo on 18 June 1815. At the time of the exhibition, the model was in the possession of a Mrs Malone of Glendruid in Cabinteely.

At the stand belonging to the Grafton Street pharmaceutical company of Hayes, Conygham & Robinson – in addition to its usual collection of perfumes and soaps – it was possible to purchase a concoction intriguingly called 'Haynes Desiccative Rat Paste'. If you needed warming up, the Bovril stand could supply you with a mug of 'normal' Bovril or Bovril lozenges and, if you fancied dessert, a product called Bovril Chocolate!

However, if there had been a prize awarded for the least -visited stand at the exhibition, it would surely have been awarded to the Dublin and Wicklow Manure Company of Annesley Bridge in Fairview which displayed several different varieties of manure at their stand.

Music played a large part in the event and a total of thirty-two bands performed in Herbert Park during the six-month period of the exhibition. The majority of these were British military bands but some local outfits such as the Dublin Operative Baker's Band, the York Street Workman's Club Band and the Dublin Total Abstinence Working Man's Band also performed at the event.

After the exhibition had finished, all of the buildings were sold off to various interests within two years and the park was eventually thrown open to the public.

Bleeding Horse

The Bleeding Horse at the top of Camden Street is one of Dublin's oldest pubs – it has been there for at least 300 years, and probably longer. There have been a number of legends concerning the name of the pub over the years, the most persistent being that it became the Bleeding Horse after the Battle of Rathmines in 1649, when horses that had been injured in the fighting were treated there.

This suggestion does have some merit as there were a huge number of horses used in the battle between the Royalist Army led by the duke of Ormonde and the Parliamentarians, who were under the command of Colonel Michael Jones. Ormonde suffered a devastating defeat at the Battle of Rathmines which culminated in him fleeing in the direction of Kildare with the remnants of his bloodied and beaten forces. Ormonde's ignominious retreat was said to have been covered by his cavalry detachment of 1,000 horses.

Contemporary accounts of the engagement say that Ormonde barely managed to escape from Rathmines with his life by jumping his horse over a ditch, so perhaps the Bleeding Horse was named in connection with these events.

It has also been suggested that the name originated from the old practice of horses being bled as a remedy for all kinds of equine diseases. One British 'bleeder' called White, known as 'Bleed' em White', said of the practice in 1825: 'In almost all the internal diseases of horses, bleeding is the essential remedy; and the earlier and more freely it is employed, the more effectually will it generally be found.'

Horses were generally bled from the jugular vein in the neck and a sign depicting a horse with a bleeding neck hung over the door of the pub for many years.

The Bleeding Horse features prominently in Dublin writer, Joseph Sheridan Le Fanu's novel *The Cock and the Anchor*, published in 1845, in which he gave the following description of the establishment:

> Some time within the first ten years of the eighteenth century, there stood at the southern extremity of the city, near the point at which Camden Street now terminates, a small, old-fashioned building, something between an ale-house and an inn. It occupied the roadside by no means unpicturesquely; one gable jutted into the road, with a projecting window, which stood out from the building like a glass box held together by a massive frame of wood.

Le Fanu also described a painted sign similar to the one mentioned above which hung over the inn door. The sign, according to Le Fanu, represented a white horse, out of whose neck there spouted a crimson cascade and underneath, in large letters, the traveller was informed that this was the genuine old Bleeding Horse.

Le Fanu goes on to describe the scene when a shady character called 'Brimstone Bill' and his companion arrived at the inn, entered the stable yard at the back and entrusted their horses to the care of a ragged stable boy. 'The lesser of the two men, leaving his companion in the passage, opened a door, within which were a few fellows drowsily toping, and one or two asleep.'

The Bleeding Horse also features in James Joyce's *Ulysses* and Joyce himself was known to visit the bar on occasion. The pub is mentioned in 'Nighttown' when Corley says to Stephen Dedalus, 'Who's that with you?'

'I saw him a few times in the Bleeding Horse in Camden Street with Boylan the billsticker,' replied Dedalus. The poet James Clarence Mangan was also a frequent visitor to the bar, as was Oliver St John Gogarty and Sean O'Casey.

Madame Tussaud

Almost 250 years after her birth in Strasbourg, Madame Tussaud is still world famous as a wax model exhibitor. But what is not so well known is the fact that she spent four years of her illustrious career based in Dublin.

Tussaud was born Marie Grosholtz, daughter of Johannes Grosholtz and Anna Maria Walder of Strasbourg in 1760 and her father died before she was born. Her mother then took up a post as housekeeper to a young doctor in Berne, Switzerland. Dr Philippe Curtius was a medical doctor who had taken to moulding wax figures to help with his anatomical studies. Curtius soon realised that his talents lay in the artistic world rather than the medical and he also found it to be a much more lucrative vocation.

He moved to Paris where he opened a small waxworks museum and he took the young Marie on as a trainee. She learned quickly and by the age of eighteen, Marie was making wax models of luminaries such as the French philosopher, Voltaire, and she was also employed as art tutor to a sister of Louis XVI.

When the French Revolution broke out in 1789 Curtius and Marie were commissioned to make models of some of the leading members of French society who had met their end on the guillotine.

Curtius died in 1794 leaving his entire waxwork collection to Marie. She married Francois Tussaud the following year. In 1802 she entered into a partnership with a man called Philipstal, who owned a travelling exhibition known as the 'Phantasmagoria' and they launched a joint exhibition at the Lyceum Theatre in London in 1803.

Following a successful stint in Edinburgh and Glasgow, Madame Tussaud and her son Joseph set sail for Dublin in February 1804 and moved into lodgings at 16 Clarendon Street. She bought out her partner M. Philipstal's share of the business and established an exhibition at Shakespeare's Gallery in Exchequer Street.

Madame Tussaud was evidently pleased with her reception in Dublin as she wrote to her family back in Paris: ' … everything is going well. When I am in Dublin the takings can reach £100 sterling a month. People come in crowds every day from 6 o'clock until 10 o'clock …'

Madame Tussaud decided to take her exhibition on a tour of Ireland and she quite literally decided to 'test the water' by travelling to Waterford by sea. On the return trip to Dublin, three ships carrying wax exhibits left Waterford at the same time as the one that Madame Tussaud was travelling on and sank within minutes of leaving the harbour. Although she was uninjured, many of her wax figures were broken and she returned to Dublin where she spent several months repairing and replacing the damaged exhibits.

She remained in Dublin with her Exchequer Street Exhibition which continued to attract the interest of Dubliners until the spring of 1805. She then took her show on the road again, visiting Cork, Limerick, Galway, Kilkenny, Mullingar and Belfast before returning to Scotland in July of 1808.

Madame Tussaud had made plans to return to Dublin with her exhibition in 1821 to coincide with a visit to Ireland by King George IV. She left Liverpool on board *The Earl of Moira* in August of that year but the ship was wrecked not long after it had left Liverpool. Madame Tussaud and her companions were rescued, but many of her precious wax exhibits were washed overboard. Madame Tussaud returned to Liverpool and she never set foot in Ireland again. She died in 1850 at the age of ninety.

Liffey Ferry

When the last remaining Liffey ferry made its final journey across the river on 20 October 1984, it brought to an end a tradition that had lasted for at least 700 years. The first documentary evidence of a ferry on the Liffey is found in the *Calendar of Ancient Records of Dublin*. Richard II granted to the mayor and citizens of Dublin in 1385, the use of a ferry for a period of four years on the site of the old bridge of Dublin, which had fallen down. The profits from the ferry were to be invested in the re-building of the bridge and the fare was one farthing for each human passenger and a halfpenny for cows and horses rated at twelve pence value and above. Sheep and pigs (dead or alive) were charged a farthing and anything else was negotiable.

The next mention of a ferry on the Liffey came in 1624 in the Dublin Assembly Roll: when it was recorded that 'Richard Golburne, merchant, shall alone be licensed to keep a ferry during his natural life on the river of Annaliffe ... paying to the city yearly five shillings, and that none shall have a ferry there without the consent of the table of aldermen ...'

In 1634 the assembly was up in arms over a decision imposed on them by the English lord deputy to 'putt one Amby in possession of the ferry belonging unto this citty, whereby the citty has been altogether dispossessed thereof'. We don't know who Amby was, but the city threatened to take the matter to court. However, no further action was taken and the matter appears to have been resolved amicably.

By 1652 the rights to the Liffey ferry had been granted to one Nathaniel Fowkes, a Dublin tailor. He was granted rights to the ferry which he was to supply himself 'for the rest of his natural life' at an annual rate of 8 pounds and 10 shillings. In 1666 Fowkes obtained a ninety-nine year lease of the ferries for the sum of 10 pounds per year.

His monopoly of the ferries seems to have been resented in some quarters by 1669. Fowkes – by now an alderman himself – made an unsuccessful attempt to get the assembly to take action against named persons who were interfering with his business. Fowkes complained that his 'boats are dayly stopt and interrupted by Mr Mabbott and colonel Carey Dillon and others'.

In 1670, the building of a wooden bridge across the Liffey at the bottom of Watling Street (now Rory O'More Bridge) caused controversy because it created competition for the owners of a ferry in the immediate vicinity. The owners arranged for a large group of apprentices to tear the bridge down, but twenty of them were arrested and taken to Dublin Castle. The apprentices were later transferred to the Bridewell but four of them were killed during a rescue attempt. From then on the bridge became known as the 'Bloody Bridge'. Several attempts were made to change the name to 'Barrack Bridge' but it continued to be known locally as the 'Bloody Bridge'.

During the early part of the nineteenth century, William Walsh – who built the Ha'penny Bridge with John Beresford – owned the lease on the Liffey ferries. The lease ran out in 1915 and control of the ferries reverted to Dublin Corporation. In 1920 the corporation installed a new ferry service using motorised boats and this service continued until 20 October 1984 when it was closed down.

Joseph Damer

Before the advent of banking institutions such as the Bank of Ireland, the financial needs of Dublin's merchants and the upper classes were met by the many private banks then operating in the city.

One of the earliest of these banks had its headquarters at the London Tavern in Fishamble Street. This was described in 1667 as 'a timber house slated, a base court, a back building more backward, and a small garden in Fishamble Street'.

It was to this salubrious establishment that Joseph Damer, a wealthy young man and former soldier of Oliver Cromwell's Parliamentary army arrived in 1662 and he rented a room from landlord George Hewlett, a former sheriff of Dublin.

Damer embarked on what was to become a very lucrative and profitable career in the banking and money-lending business. He initially bought a large property in Thurles, Co. Tipperary and stocked it with 10,000 sheep and he also established a candle-making business near Cashel. As soon as his Tipperary business ventures were up and running, Damer brought his nephew over from England to take charge and he returned to the London Tavern where he began to concentrate on his banking business.

Damer's activities soon came to the attention of Jonathan Swift, who loathed moneylenders and bankers and he seems to have taken a particular dislike to Damer. So much so, that when Damer died, Swift and his friends composed a very unflattering elegy to the dead banker:

He walked the streets, and wore a threadbare cloak;
He dined and supped at charge of other folk;
And by his looks, had he held out his palms,
He might be thought an object fit for alms.
Oh! London Tavern, thou hast lost a friend,
Though in thy walls he ne'er did farthing spend ...

Damer died at an advanced age in 1720 and the following obituary appeared in *Whalley's Newsletter* on 11 July of that year, which contradicted Swift's view of him: 'On Wednesday last Mr Joseph Deamer [sic] died at his house in Smithfield upwards of ninety years of age, with not above £340,000, and last night was interred in St Paul's church in Oxmantown Green attended by a numerous train of gentlemen's as well as by hackney coaches ... I knew him upwards of fifty years, and though his fortune was all his own acquiring I believe that it was every penny got honestly. His purse was open to all he believed to be honest or where he thought his money secure ...'

He had the reputation of being a miser but it emerged later that Damer had given away a great deal of money to deserving causes during his lifetime and funded several charities in the city. He was a member of the Unitarian Church and he funded a charity school attached to the Unitarian church on Stephen's Green. This establishment was called the Damer School in his honour and it continued to receive funding from his estate until well into the twentieth century.

Damer also established a house of refuge at 27 Parnell Street for the destitute Protestant widows of St Mary's parish.

The refuge catered for twenty widows, housing them in their own rooms and providing them with a weekly allowance of food, fuel and a small amount of spending money.

Star-shaped Fort

The names of Bernard De Gomme and 'Honest Tom' Philips are not ones that immediately spring to mind in connection with the development of Dublin, but if these military engineers had had their way back in the late 1600s, the south-east inner city area of Dublin might have looked a little bit different to the way it looks today.

Following an audacious attack on the British Navy by the Dutch fleet in 1667 on the River Thames, during which several English warships were destroyed, the English government scuttled thirteen ships in the river to act as a temporary blockade while plans were made to strengthen existing defences.

Sir Bernard De Gomme, described as 'his majesties chief engineer', was ordered to put together a plan for the defence of the Thames and he drew up plans to construct a star-shaped fort at Tilbury on the river.

The star-shaped fort design was all the rage in Europe at the time and it was particularly in vogue with French military engineers. These pentagonal defensive structures, surrounded by straight-sided moats, were designed to have an all-round view, eliminating any possible blind spots from which attacks could be launched.

In 1672 De Gomme was ordered to Dublin to perform a similar task and he decided to design a huge citadel at the mouth of the Liffey for the defence of the city. In his report to Charles II, De Gomme proposed to build his citadel at Ringsend and link it to the city by the construction of a causeway leading from Ringsend to Lazy Hill (Townsend Street).

This massive star-shaped construction was to be built on the same principles as De Gomme's Tilbury Fort on the Thames. Had it been built, the fort would have covered an area of thirty acres and would have been capable of accommodating seven hundred soldiers and officers. Like Tilbury the plan was to incorporate a prison, a chapel, a house for the governor and a large gateway with a drawbridge.

De Gomme proposed to centre this new fort on an existing defensive tower in the middle of Ringsend and if his proposal had gone ahead, the whole village as we know it today and a large portion of the surrounding area would have been obliterated.

The scheme never got off the ground, possibly due to the projected cost of over £130,000, which was an enormous amount of money for those times. The cost of building the similar but much smaller-scale Charles Fort in Kinsale, which was built during the same era, only came to just over £10,000.

Following De Gomme's death in 1685 the idea to build a citadel was resurrected by 'Honest Tom' Philips who suggested a different location for the fortification. Philips had worked with De Gomme on the original map and plan in 1673.

Philips' proposed citadel was quite similar to De Gomme's but he suggested that it be built close to where Merrion Square is now located. It must be borne in mind that the seashore in those days came very close to Merrion Square.

If Philips' scheme had gone ahead, the citadel would have been built over an extensive area of Dublin centred on Merrion Square, Fitzwilliam Square, Baggot Street and Mount Street Upper and Lower.

This grandiose scheme also came to nothing, which was just as well. Many other European cities had invested heavily in this type of fortification only to find them rendered useless by advances in heavy artillery and ammunition.

A fort was eventually built at the Pigeon House harbour but on nowhere near the massive scale that had been envisaged by De Gomme and Philips.

Linen Hall

The street names of Linenhall Street and Yarnhall Street off Bolton Street are today the only reminders that for much of the eighteenth century Dublin was of central importance to the country's linen trade.

Linen weaving has been a feature of Irish life from as far back as the late Bronze Age and it was a particularly important industry during the eighteenth and nineteenth centuries. In those days the manufacture of linen in Ireland was a cottage industry and it provided a regular source of income for families in rural areas throughout Ireland.

The first Linen Board was established in 1711 in order to control the sale of linen and it was originally based in a small rented room on Cork Hill.

At a meeting of the Linen Board on St Patrick's Day in 1722 the question of building a centralised Linen Hall was addressed and several prospective sites around the city were considered. One or two sites in Drumcondra were looked at and duly rejected on the basis that they were too far away from the city and more importantly from the Liffey. Another site near Ballybough was rejected for the same reason.

Another site that was given serious consideration was the 'Little Green' where the 'new' Newgate Prison was erected many years afterwards in 1780.

The Board eventually came down in favour of a three-acre site located at the top of Capel Street, which was then on the perimeter of the city. This particular site was chosen because of its proximity to the inns and taverns on Church Street and Pill Lane, where many linen traders lodged while on business in Dublin.

Over the course of the next six years the Linen Hall gradually took shape and it opened for trade on 14 November 1728.

The Dublin Linen Hall was modelled on the famous Cloth Hall of Hamburg and the great London market, Blackwell Hill. The Linen Hall contained a large trading floor and 550 compartments or bays for the storage of linen. There was also a large boardroom for the use of the trustees and what was described as 'a large and elegant coffee-room for the accommodation of factors and traders who daily crowd its courts'.

Security was tight in the Linen Hall. The market began and ended with the ringing of a large bell and anyone still on the premises after closing time was liable to be kept there overnight. The whole operation was overseen by a chamberlain whose main task was to look after the hundreds of keys required for the Linen Hall's numerous linen lockers and chambers. Other staff included a uniformed gate-keeper, a clerk and several porters. During the night the premises were guarded by night watchmen who were issued with firearms.

With the opening of the Belfast Linen Hall in 1783 the Dublin industry went into terminal decline and the Linen Board was abolished in 1828. Thackeray, in his *Irish Sketch Book*, described a visit to the Linen Hall which was in a near -derelict state in 1842: 'I need not say how we went to see the Linen Hall of Dublin, that huge, useless, lonely, decayed place in the vast solitude of which stands the simpering statue of George IV. Pointing to some bales of shirting, over which, he is supposed to extend his august protection.'

During the 1870s the Linen Hall was used as a temporary barracks by the British Army and it was taken over by the board of works in 1878. One of the last events held in the Linen Hall was the Dublin Civic Exhibition of 1914. It was destroyed by fire during the 1916 Rebellion.

Theatre Riots

On the night of 14 December 1822, the famous Theatre Royal in Hawkins Street was the scene of a riot, known afterwards as 'The Bottle Row', which resulted in four Dublin Orangemen being charged with the attempted murder of the duke of Wellington. This seems to have been a complete overreaction by Dublin Castle as only one missile was reported to have struck the duke's box and a bottle and several sticks were thrown around the theatre.

The four accused were George Graham, Henry Hanbridge or Handwich, his brother Matthew and James Forbes and at least half a dozen other were charged with riotous assembly.

The men, all with addresses in Hawkins Street, were accused of hooting, groaning and hissing at the lord lieutenant, and showering him with sticks, copper pipes and a wide variety of empty glass bottles. Even more seriously, they were charged with conspiracy to 'kill and murder his Excellency, Richard Marquis Wellesley, Lord Lieutenant of Ireland'.

The accused men had decided to stage a protest against Wellesley because he had earlier voiced his disapproval of the practice of decorating King Billy's (William of Orange) statue in College Green with Orange sashes on the anniversary of his arrival in Ireland. They were also demonstrating against the lord mayor of Dublin, John Fleming, who had banned the practice some weeks earlier.

The Orangemen had managed to get their hands on one hundred tickets for the play and they kept quiet until the interval when they produced handbills denouncing Wellesley and Fleming with slogans such as, 'Fleming, although he has the mace, may find it hard to keep his place', as well as the standard 'No Popery' placards.

There was also a great deal of shouting and singing of Orange songs during the 'row' but very little occurred in the way of physical violence. All four men were eventually acquitted.

Six years earlier on 16 December 1814, another lord lieutenant was caught up in a Dublin theatre riot. The venue on that occasion was Crow Street theatre in Temple Bar and the riot that occurred became known afterwards as 'The Dog Row'.

The lord lieutenant had gone to Crow Street to see the popular and long-running play *Forest of Bondy* and he particularly wanted to see the star of the show *The Dog of Montargis* played by a Dublin canine thespian called Dragon. However, on the night in question, Dragon's master decided to strike for a better pay deal. The irate manager told him where to go, so dog and master quite literally 'got off the stage' and left the theatre.

The manager hurriedly arranged to put on a substitute play and all seemed well until the end of the show when one of the manager's underlings went on stage to apologise for the non-appearance of Dragon.

The speech failed to satisfy the rowdies in the cheap seats and they called on the manager to come out and face them himself. No amount of cajoling could force him from his hiding-place backstage, so the angry mob proceeded to wreck the theatre.

The lord lieutenant and his entourage were forced to flee from Crow Street while the crowd went berserk. The lord lieutenant's box was torn asunder, chandeliers were smashed to pieces while the rioters up in the galleries broke up benches and threw them on top of the musicians in the pit. The theatre never fully recovered from this incident and following another major riot five years later, Crow Street closed its doors for the last time.

William Street

In his *Dublin Street Names*, C.T. McCready states that South William Street was named after King William III soon after the battle of the Boyne but this is not the case. South William Street actually takes its name from William Williams, who developed it along with Clarendon Street and the Clarendon Market during the 1670s.

The Dublin Assembly Roll for 1671 states that Williams 'shall have a new lease of a plot situate on Hoggen Green, continuing from the end of Trinity Hall to the brick chimney belonging to John Sams House …' Williams was given the land by Dublin Corporation on a lease of ninety-nine years for the princely sum of eight pounds sterling per annum and 'a couple of fat capons' for the lord mayor at Christmas.

The area leased by Williams was also referred to as being 'neere Tibb and Tom' in other corporation documents. The name 'Tibb and Tom' appears to describe an area on Hoggen Green mentioned by Walter Harris in his *History and*

Antiquities of the City of Dublin where, according to Harris there was 'a small range of buildings called Tibb and Tom where possibly the citizens amused themselves at leisure by playing at Keals or ninepins'. Gilbert also describes Tibb and Tom as 'a range of buildings' beside the Hoggen Butts where Dubliners honed their archery skills.

Today the street is dominated by the magnificent Powerscourt House, which was built between 1771 and 1774. The house was built by Richard Wingfield, third Viscount Powerscourt and it was one of the largest dwelling houses in Dublin. The house – which cost £8,000 to build – was designed by a James' Street stonemason Robert Mack. The house was built using Wicklow granite from the Powerscourt Estate and it was complete by 1774. However, it was only used as the Wingfield's city residence until 1807 when it was sold to the government for £15,000.

One of the street's most interesting buildings is 58 South William Street. It was built in 1765 by the Society of Artists which held its first exhibition there the following year, featuring well-known artists of the day, such as Gabriel Beranger, Bernard Scale, Somervil Pope, Peter Shee and Jeremiah Barrett. The society continued to hold exhibitions at the hall until 1780 by which time most of its members had emigrated to London.

Richard Cranfield, owner of Cranfield's Baths in Irishtown, then took over the lease of the building and it continued to host plays and concerts and was a popular venue for all manner of exhibitions.

In 1791 the Exhibition Rooms became the City Assembly House. The Tholsel in High Street was in imminent danger of collapse, so Dublin Corporation arranged to rent the premises from Cranfield at fifty guineas per annum. When Cranfield died in 1809 the corporation bought his interest in the building and occupied it until 1852 when the Assembly moved to City Hall.

When a new city fire service was established in 1862 the basement of the City Assembly House was used as a fire station. The station housed nine firemen and one small engine until 1885 when it transferred to Chatham Row. Today the building is in use as the Dublin Civic Museum and is home to the Old Dublin Society.

Monto

Dublin's infamous 'Monto' district immortalised in the song 'Take Me up to Monto' and in James Joyce's *Ulysses* as 'Nighttown' was once the biggest and best-known brothel district in Europe. During its heyday it was estimated that there were 1,600 prostitutes working there at any given time. One Dublin judge commenting on the area in 1901 described Monto as 'one of the most dreadful dens of immorality in Europe'.

Monto was so famous that it was even mentioned in an edition of the *Encyclopedia Britannica* in an article on prostitution: 'Dublin furnishes an exception to the usual practice in the United Kingdom. In that city police permit open houses confined to one street, but carried on more publicly than even in the south of Europe or Algeria.'

Monto takes its name from Montgomery Street (now Foley Street) but the most notorious street in the area was Mecklenburgh Street. There were also a large number of smaller brothels and shebeens in the surrounding streets and laneways such as those found at Purdon Street, Mabbot Street, Elliott Place, Faithful Place and Beaver Street.

North inner city Dublin folklorist and local historian Terry Fagan was born and bred in the heart of Monto and has written a comprehensive and detailed history of the area entitled *Monto - Madams, Murder and Black Coddle*. Fagan says that Monto, which was also known locally as 'The Kips', 'The Digs' and 'The Village', 'became the undisputed centre of attraction for those in search of Dublin's alternative nightlife.' Mecklenburgh Street, which was the hub of the district, according to Fagan, 'was set up to cater for the needs of punters of all classes. The higher numbers in the street were where the so-called "flash houses" were to be found. These houses catered for a higher class of customer. The lower numbers were where the less-well off were catered for.'

The large number of soldiers living in close proximity to Monto kept trade in the area flourishing for many years. In addition, the port of Dublin was also thriving and for many sailors arriving in Dublin, Monto was their first port of call. Inevitably, many of Monto's women and their clients succumbed to the ravages of venereal disease.

During the last twenty years of the nineteenth century, the spread of sexually transmitted diseases was rampant in Dublin and in 1880 it was estimated that over 30 per cent of the British Army's 5,000-strong Dublin garrison was infected. In 1881 one British Army commander complained that half the unmarried men in his regiment had succumbed to venereal disease.

Of course, large numbers of Monto's working women ended up suffering from these diseases themselves and the Westmoreland Lock Hospital for venereal disease in Townsend Street was the last refuge for many of them.

The brothels went into decline after the First World War and following the departure of the British Army in 1922 the writing was on the wall for Monto. The end of the red light district was hastened by a vigorous campaign led by Frank Duff and the Legion of Mary. The end for Monto came on the night of 12 March 1925 when gardaí launched a massive raid on the remaining brothels in the area. Over one hundred women and their clients were arrested and those detained were taken to Store Street Garda Station. Their number included a Donegal TD who protested that he had only been there for a drink.

The Poddle

The River Poddle has been known by several different names over the centuries such as the Puddle, Pottle and the Podell. It was known by some as the Tiber and also as the Salach, meaning 'dirty', or the Soulagh. This latter name has been immortalised by the Dubliners in the song 'Down by the River Saile'.

The Poddle which rises in Tallaght was at one time, the main source of fresh water for the medieval city of Dublin.

As the city expanded the demand for water increased accordingly and in April 1244 Maurice Fitzgerald, justiciar of Ireland, commanded the sheriff of Dublin 'without delay … to make inquisition, with advice of the Mayor and citizens, as to whence water can be best and most conveniently taken from its course and conducted to the King's city of Dublin, for the benefit of the city, and at the cost of the citizens.'

To this end, Dublin Corporation entered into an agreement with the Abbey of St Thomas, which owned the rights to the Dodder at Balrothery, to re-route water from the Dodder into the Poddle. The water was diverted by way of a two mile man-made canal that came to be known as the 'City Watercourse' and which remained in use until 1775. Parts of this watercourse can still be seen today in the Dodder Valley Linear Park near Tallaght.

The Poddle, which is now mostly underground, flows into Dublin via Templeogue and Kimmage where the river divides into two at a place called the Tongue near Mount Argus. One strand, which supplied the City Watercourse, flows down through the Liberties and the other flows through Harold's Cross. The two streams reunite at the junction of Patrick's Street and Dean Street. It then flows past the cathedral, turns east and flows down under Ship Street and Dublin Castle to merge with the Liffey at Wellington Quay.

St Patrick's Cathedral is built on a small island between the two strands of the Poddle that is referred to in a document written in 1179 as 'St Patrick's in insula' or St Patrick's on the island. There was also a holy well dedicated to the saint on the island and this is now covered over by the park adjoining the cathedral. Legend has it that Patrick himself performed baptisms at this well.

This stretch of the Poddle was very prone to flooding and the cathedral was inundated many times over the centuries. In 1687 it was reported that the floodwater in the cathedral rose above the level of the desks and on another occasion it was flooded to a depth of five feet while boats sailed on the swollen river outside.

The present-day junction of Dean Street and Patrick's Street was, until 200 years ago, called Cross Poddle. This was obviously one of the main crossing points over the Poddle either by way of a bridge or ford and was the place where local women gathered to wash clothes.

It is not clear when exactly the name of Soulagh or Salach was applied to the Poddle but there were certainly many reports written over the centuries in relation to the filthy state of the river. The main culprits seem to have been the many industries and mills that lined the banks of the river and contaminated the water with bleach, refuse from the skinners' yards and other materials, rendering the water undrinkable. The city section of the river was eventually covered over during the eighteenth century in an effort to keep the water clean.

Brass Money

When James II abdicated from the English throne in December 1688 he went to France for a while but he returned to Ireland in March 1689 in an attempt to regain his throne. James urgently needed money to fund his campaign and on the following day he issued a decree raising the value of English gold by 20 per cent and silver by 8 per cent.

By June of that year James was still short of money so he decided to make his own out of brass and he established mints at the Deanery in Limerick and at 27 Capel Street in Dublin to make sixpences, shillings and half crowns. James' proclamation of 18 June 1689 read: 'Whereas, for remedy of the present scarcity of money in this our kingdom, and that our standing forces may be the better paid and subsisted, and that our subjects of this realm may be the better enabled to pay and discharge the taxes, excise, customs, rents, and other debts and duties, which are or shall be hereafter payable to us; we have ordered a certain quantity of copper and brass money to be coined to pass in this our kingdom during our pleasure ...'

The manufacture of brass money was only intended to be a temporary measure and the coins were dated by month as well as year because James had planned to convert them into silver on a month-by-month basis once he was back on the throne, but this obviously never happened.

The Capel Street mint contained two coin presses: one was called the 'James Press' and the other was 'the Duchess'. The mint worked twenty-four hours a day to keep up with the demand for coin and staff working on the presses worked twelve-hour shifts in order to keep the operation going.

The mint soon ran out of copper and brass and the sourcing of new metals became an urgent priority. The mint commissioners embarked on a country-wide search for brass and copper. Later on, when these materials became scarce, tin and pewter were used in the manufacture of the coins.

A certain amount of desperation seemed to be setting in, judging by an order sent out by the commissioners in July 1689 commanding the authorities at Dublin Castle to deliver to the mint at Capel Street 'those two brass canons now lying in the court of this our castle ...'

In January of the following year the castle received a large quantity of mixed metals from Walter Plunkett in Limerick which contained 'six hundred weight of gunn mettle' and a similar amount of pewter. He also promised to send in the next consignment, four or five broken bells and a number of useless cannons from Galway and Kinsale. The use of old brass cannons in the manufacture of the coins gave rise to the new currency being known popularly as 'gun money'.

In June 1690, the situation became so bad that all half-crowns were recalled to the mint and were re-struck as crowns while other coins were reduced in size to save metal. A small amount of pewter pennies and halfpennies were also struck along with a small quantity of white metal crowns and half-crowns.

James had fled Ireland following the Battle of the Boyne and the Capel Street mint fell into the hands of the Williamite forces. One of William III's earliest proclamations from his camp at Finglas just after the battle in 1690 devalued the brass and copper coinage to a fraction of its value and in February 1691 the currency was declared to be worthless.

Black Death

Dublin suffered from many natural disasters during the Middle Ages but none was worse than the dreaded bubonic plague or 'Black Death' that swept through Europe in the middle of the fourteenth century. The bubonic plague spread to humans from fleas carried by black rats that lived in the holds of the thousands of merchant ships travelling between different ports.

The Black Death – so called because it produced black spots on the skin – was first seen in China during the 1330s and it later spread to the rest of Asia and then into Europe. Once the disease reached Europe it was only a matter of time until it reached Ireland, which it duly did in August 1348.

The Kilkenny-based Franciscan, Friar Clyn provides us with one of the few detailed descriptions of the effects of the Black Death in Dublin. According to Clyn the plague first arrived at Howth or Dalkey and quickly spread to the rest of the city and to Drogheda. The friar claimed that the disease killed 14,000 people in Dublin before Christmas: 'There was hardly a house in which one only had died but as a rule man and wife with their children and all the family went the common way of death.' Clyn's estimate seems quite high and could possibly have been exaggerated but there is no way today that the friar's claims can be verified.

Clyn also recorded that: 'Many died from carbuncles and boils and buboes which grew on the legs and under the arms, others from passion of the head, as if thrown into a frenzy; others by vomiting blood.' Clyn succumbed to the disease himself, as evidenced by the final entry in the friar's account of the disaster: 'I leave parchment for continuing this work if happily any man survive and any of the race of Adam escape the pestilence and carry on the work which I have begun.' Some unknown scribe added a footnote to the document some time later with the words: 'Here it seems that the author died.'

Following the disaster of 1348, the disease continued to smoulder for some years and there were further outbreaks over the course of the next three centuries, which led to many deaths in Dublin. There were two more outbreaks in the city before the end of the fourteenth century and it was devastated by the Black Death in 1439. Three thousand citizens were said to have perished during that outbreak.

There were four serious plague epidemics during the sixteenth century, including one that began in 1519 and didn't disappear until 1525. Again, this outbreak resulted in a high mortality rate and many were reported to have fled the city for the relative safety of the surrounding countryside.

There was another major incidence of the disease in 1650 and 1651, which led to huge loss of life and a sharp decrease in the population of Dublin. This was the last major occurrence of the Black Death in Dublin, although isolated cases were reported for many years afterwards.

One would imagine that, given the huge scale of the tragedy in Dublin, mass plague graves would have been uncovered before now but to date this has not been the case. Some smaller burial pits, such as those uncovered at Crow Street and at Swords, have been tentatively linked to the Black Death but no large-scale burial grounds have been found. It has been suggested in the past that there were mass graves at Blackpitts off the South Circular Road, but this rumour hasn't been backed up by any physical evidence.

Grievance Association

In August 1847, DMP Inspector John Flint, secretary of a body called The Dublin Police Grievance Association, presented a report to the lord lieutenant of Ireland. The report contained a short history of the Dublin Metropolitan Police and a number of general observations in relation to police manning levels, pay and pensions and a large number of issues generally related to the policing of crime in Dublin over the course of the previous eleven years.

For the most part the report is of a fairly mundane nature, detailing day-to-day issues associated with the policing of a large city like Dublin but now and again Flint's report (without meaning to) provides us with some fascinating and often humorous glimpses of what life must have been like in the city during the period leading up to the Great Famine.

Commenting on the sometimes infirm nature of some of the old watchmen policing in Dublin prior to the formation of the DMP, Flint details the case of a character named 'Badojos Kavanagh'. Kavanagh had apparently been a member of the old parish watch and was taken into the DMP despite having lost one of his hands some years earlier. The lack of a hand was only discovered a few years later when Badojos fell sick on the job and a police doctor tried to take his pulse. When the doctor asked Kavanagh who had passed him as fit for duty he replied, 'You did!'

Flint's report also contains an interesting table which gives an analysis of 257 dismissals from the DMP between April 1838 and January 1839. The vast majority of the dismissals were drink-related: thirty members were dismissed for being drunk on the beat, eleven for being drunk in bed, nine for being drunk in a brothel, two for being drunk and quarrelling with the artillery and four for being found 'Drunk asleep in a covered car'.

One member was dismissed for double-jobbing, being found 'in an oyster shop inviting persons to enter', another for 'lying on a guard-bed with a female and [being] abusive' while two others were thrown out for being 'found in a brothel with uniform on'.

In the event of being assaulted in the course of duty, DMP men were entitled to compensation for their injuries. One constable, Owen Carolan, was dismissed in December 1838 for 'cutting his great coat, belt and blue coat and pretending himself stabbed'.

Flint also mentions the exploits of the fire police division of the DMP, which seems to have been the Dublin version of the 'Keystone Cops'. Flint said this particular branch of the DMP 'has proved itself an utterly inefficient body as a Fire Police ... wretched management and bad judgement has been shown at all our fires; there have been too many officers giving instructions, each urging his own crude plan ...'

Flint acknowledged that while many members of the Fire Police showed great personal courage, others were often found to be drunk while attending fires and he mentioned one particular incident that took place during a fire in Dorset Street on 7 January 1839.

An inquiry established afterwards that while 'a great number of men behaved in an exemplary manner at the fire in Dorset Street; they regret to say that many cases of intoxication took place at that fire'.

Three police constables, Thomas Holland, Joseph Burn and Jacob Doyle were found drunk in the cellar of a burning house in Dorset Street while their comrades were outside fighting the fire. Holland and one of the other constables were found to have stolen four bottles of wine from the cellar. The three men were dismissed from the force the following day but were reinstated just two weeks later.

St Audoen's

Just inside the last remaining gate and archway of the old walled city of Dublin, at the top of 'the forty steps' is St Audoen's church in High Street, which is one of Dublin's oldest churches. The present building was constructed sometime around 1190, but it has been suggested that this was built on the site of a much earlier church. The church, built in honour of Audoen or Owen, the seventh-century patron saint of Normandy, is the oldest medieval parish church in Dublin still in use today.

The church was associated with the guilds of the city for many years and it had a particular association with the guild of St Anne, which was authorised to build a chapel dedicated to the memory of the saint in 1430. St Audoen's Arch, also called the 'Town's Arch', was also an established meeting place for several other Dublin guilds such as those of the smiths, butchers, bakers, bricklayers and the feltmakers. The meetings were held in a tower over St Audoen's Arch.

John Gilbert informs us that in 1755 Reverend Cobbe, rector of St Audoen's, for some reason removed the cross from the church steeple and had it replaced with a boar's head wearing a crown, which led to the following verse believed to have been penned by Jonathan Swift:

Christ's Cross from Christ's church cursed Cobbe hath plucked down,
And placed in its stead what he worships – the Crown.
Avenging the cause of the Gadarene People,
The miscreant hath placed a swine's head on the steeple;
By this intimating to all who pass by,
That his hearers are swine, and his church but a stye.

The main evidence that there was an earlier church on the site of St Audoen's is provided by an ancient gravestone situated just inside the main door of St Audoen's. The gravestone, known as the 'Lucky Stone', dates from the seventh or eighth century and has a long association with St Audoen's.

The Lucky Stone was believed to have magical properties and in medieval times many queued to touch the stone or kiss it in the hope of gaining a cure from illness or good fortune. It has been written that many High Street merchants and traders who believed that it brought good fortune to their businesses, visited the stone daily 'which they kissed and thus a portion of the stone became smooth and polished.'

During the early part of the fourteenth century, John le Decer, lord mayor of Dublin, erected a drinking fountain in the Cornmarket and had the stone placed beside it.

Over the centuries, the Lucky Stone has gone on walkabout on occasion but has always returned to St Audoen's. It went missing for a while in 1826 but later turned up on a building site in Kilmainham. It was apparently spotted by a watchman who reported that he had seen the stone glow and assume human form after nightfall. Workmen on the site also alleged that the stone cried and moaned and rocked from side to side when they tried to break it up with a sledgehammer!

Some years later the stone turned up at St Audoen's Catholic church, next door, and later found temporary homes in Glasnevin Cemetery and Whitefriar Street Church. It eventually ended up back in its original position in 1888 and the stone was finally fixed into its present position in order to prevent any more wanderings.

The Lucky Stone is still on display at St Audoen's and the church, which has undergone a complete refurbishment in recent years, now has conducted tours which are available between May and September.

Copper-Faced Jack

'Copper-Faced Jack' Scott, earl of Clonmel, lived at Harcourt Street in Dublin and he would probably be spinning in his grave today at the thought of his name being immortalised by a Harcourt Street nightclub of the same name.

Scott, the Tipperary-born hanging judge, who gained his nickname because of his ruddy complexion, was one of the nastiest but most colourful characters of eighteenth century Dublin. During a chequered career, he managed to obtain for himself the positions of solicitor-general, attorney-general, prime sergeant, lord chief justice and finally ended up as Lord Clonmel.

According to Jonah Barrington, Scott was forever making good resolutions to abstain from excessive 'snuff, sleep, swearing, gross eating, sloth, malt liquors and indolence,' and never to taste 'anything after tea but water, and wine and water at night'. These promises usually came to nothing as he still required 'a couple of able-bodied lacqueys to carry him nightly to his bed'.

Scott had a reputation for being extremely arrogant and rude, and during his career he made many enemies. One of these was John Magee, proprietor of the *Dublin Evening Post*, whom Scott had jailed on a libel charge. It was believed at the time that Clonmel bore ill-will against Magee for having personally abused him in his paper. Magee swore to get even and on his release from prison he had posters erected around Dublin informing the citizens that he intended to spend £10,000 getting even with Copper-Faced Jack.

And get even he did! Lord Clonmel owned a villa called Temple Hill near Seapoint in County Dublin. Magee bought a plot of land which was nearly under his lordship's windows and put up notices, inviting his fellow citizens to 'days of great amusement' to be held there every weekend.

Lord Cloncurry who lived nearby, attended one of these gatherings and described the mayhem that unfolded: 'Several thousand people, including the entire disposable mob of Dublin, of both sexes, assembled as the guests at an early hour in the morning, and proceeded to enjoy themselves in tents and booths erected for the occasion. A variety of sports were arranged for their amusement, such as climbing poles for prizes, running in sacks, grinning through horse-collars, asses dressed up with wigs and scarlet robes, dancing dogs in gowns and wigs as barristers, and so forth, until at length, when the crowd had obtained its maximum density, towards the afternoon, the grand scene of the day was produced.'

For the grand finale, Magee produced several slippery pigs and let them loose in the direction of Clonmel's property, announcing that if anybody could catch one, they could keep it. With that, the entire crowd set off in hot pursuit of the pigs through Lord Clonmel's beautifully manicured gardens, destroying hedges, shrubs and flower beds in the process.

While these gatherings were of great annoyance to Copper-Faced Jack, they were not riotous enough to be deemed a public nuisance as they were held on Magee's own land and the authorities refused to take any action. His lordship eventually had the last laugh when he subsequently jailed the increasingly eccentric Magee for contempt of court.

Copper-faced Jack Scott died at the age of fifty-nine on the day the '98 rebellion broke out, on 23 May 1798, and was buried at St Peter's churchyard in Aungier Street. He died as he himself described in his diary 'a helpless, ignorant, unpopular, accursed individual: forsaken by government, persecuted by parliament, hated by the bar ... and deserted by your oldest friends.'

City Scavenger

The issue of bin collections and waste disposal in Dublin is currently exercising the minds of politicians and citizens alike but the city's streets bear little or no resemblance to the highways and byways of 'dirty old Dublin' in medieval times.

In medieval Dublin there were no flush toilets and the streets were open sewers. Pigs, cattle, sheep and horses roamed freely. Butchers and fishmongers carried on their respective trades out in the open which resulted in heaps of rotting flesh being disposed of all over the city.

Responsibility for keeping the city clean was – as it still is – in the hands of the municipal corporation of Dublin and for the authorities, the problem of waste disposal was a constant one.

An important person employed by the city in its fight against grime was the City Scavenger and one of the best-known holders of this salubrious post was a Dublin widow, Kate Stronge, who inherited the job from her dead husband.

Although it was Kate's job to look after the sanitation of the city she became notorious as one who did more to clean out the pockets of its citizens than clear up the streets. The City Scavenger was allowed to extract reasonable tolls from the citizens in order to pay for the cost of cleaning the streets but during her time in office many citizens accused Kate and her hired henchmen of extortion.

Sir James Carroll, who was mayor of Dublin in 1634, complained in a letter to the British viceroy, the earl of Wentworth, about Kate's behaviour on two grounds. His first complaint was in relation to her extortion activities in the city market: 'She had but only the toll of the market granted to her, and yet she doth continually extort on poor people coming to the market with butter, eggs, cheese, wool, fish, roots, cabbages, and almost all things that come to the market, from whom she takes what she pleaseth ...'

The mayor, who wanted the viceroy to remove Kate from office, also complained about her neglect of the city streets, saying: 'She is so much affected to profit as she will never find sufficient carriage to take away the dung, for where six carts are few enough to take away the dung of the city every week to keep it clean, she did and will maintain but two, which can scarce keep the way from the castle to the church clean ...'

Concerns about the City Scavenger's behaviour had begun two years earlier with a petition to the City Assembly that Kate had emptied so much dung into the river near 'George Beddely's garden' that small boats could only approach the quay (Wood Quay) during a spring tide.

Further complaints were made against Kate and two of her agents, James Bellewe and John Butcher, again in 1634, that they were extorting payments from fish sellers and many other stall holders in the city.

Despite the complaints, the city was unable to dislodge Kate from office and she even managed to outlast the mayor of Dublin, who had complained to the viceroy about her behaviour. Sir James Carroll was removed from office and jailed for fraud and corruption in 1635.

Meanwhile, Kate continued on her merry way until 1641 when she was eventually dismissed from her post for using an illegal brass measure for taking tolls at the market.

Molyneux House

Molyneux House, which once stood at the corner of Peter Street and Bride Street, was built in 1711 by Thomas Molyneux, the first Irish State physician and physician-general to the English army in Ireland. Molyneux was born in Dublin on 14 April 1661 and he received the first part of his education at a school maintained by a Dr Henry Ryder. He graduated with a doctorate in medicine from Trinity College in 1687.

Molyneux went to live in Chester for a few years, where he practiced as a doctor, and he returned to Dublin after the Battle of the Boyne in 1690. He established a successful medical practice at his father's house in New Row in the Liberties and he later became a fellow of the College of Physicians as well as professor of medicine at Trinity.

As well as his interest in medicine, Molyneux also took a keen interest in the natural sciences and he had a particular fascination for the anatomy of animals. He published the first treatise on the anatomy of the giant Irish elk, entitled *A discourse concerning the large horns frequently found underground in Ireland*. He also wrote papers concerning insects swarming in Longford, strange outbreaks of eye diseases at Delvin, in Westmeath, and in 1715 he published a discourse on an elephant's jaw that was discovered in Cavan. Thomas' interest in elephants was shared by his brother William who wrote an account of the accidental burning to death of an elephant in Dublin in 1681.

Molyneux was married twice and he had four children from the first marriage and twelve from the second. So it's not at all surprising that he needed to build such a large house in Peter Street, which was then a very fashionable part of the city to live in. Peter Street was just a stone's throw away from the archbishop of Dublin's Palace of St Sepulchre in Kevin Street and only spitting distance from St Bride's Church where many of Molyneux's children were baptised.

When Thomas Molyneux died in 1733, various members of his family continued to live at the house in Peter Street until 1778 when Thomas' son, Capel, moved to Merrion Square.

Molyneux House – once said to have been one of the most imposing in Dublin – was later sold to an entrepreneur named Philip Astley, who wanted to build an amphitheatre close to the centre of town for his variety shows. These included 'several feats and entertainment of horsemanship, musical pieces, dancing, tumbling, and pantomime of whatever nature or sort whatever'.

It was later sold to Henry Johnstone who hoped to turn it into a theatre that would rival Smock Alley and Crow Street. When this venture ultimately failed, the property reverted to the Molyneux family. In 1815, the house was leased to a charity for the blind and it was converted to accommodate anything up to fifty blind women, while the playhouse, which had formerly housed Shakespearean actors and dancing horses, was now converted into a chapel.

The Molyneux Blind Asylum was open to all religious persuasions and catered for all ages. Those lucky enough to find a place in the asylum were taught how to make straw ropes and curtain sashes while some of the younger ones were taught to play the piano so that they could obtain work as organists at various churches around the city.

The asylum was relocated to what was regarded as a healthier location at Leeson Street in 1862 and Molyneux House was used as a hospital and by the Salvation Army, who converted it for use as a night refuge. Molyneux House was demolished in 1943 by Jacobs Biscuits, but part of the old chapel still remains and was incorporated into a new building erected on the site during the 1970s.

Kilgobbin

While the ancient south Dublin district of Kilgobbin is fast disappearing under an avalanche of house building, many relics of its fascinating past are still intact today. With its ruined castle, church and remnants of the old Pale ditch,

Kilgobbin is an oasis of antiquity in one of the city's fastest-developing suburbs.

The old church of Kilgobbin, which overlooks the village and castle of Kilgobbin, is built on the site of an earlier ecclesiastic site, believed to originate from as early as the seventh century. Not an awful lot is known about the origins of the founder of the church but Ball, in his *History of the County Dublin*, states that it was founded by St Gobban, who is mentioned in *The Martyrology of Tallaght* and *The Martyrology of Donegal*. Another legend suggests that the church was linked with the famous Gobán Saor, the master-builder of Irish mythology, who is said to have been the builder of many churches and monastic settlements throughout Ireland.

There was a church on the site during the twelfth century which was referred to as *Teach na Breathnach*, which has been translated as 'the house of the Welshmen', perhaps signifying the presence of a settlement of Welsh monks on the site.

The ruins of the most recent church built on the site nearly 300 years ago can still be seen today. There are two old graveyards in the immediate vicinity of the church. Just beside the entrance to the older one stand the remains of a granite high-cross which bears features similar to other Christian crosses that date from the ninth or tenth century. The cross was originally found inside the churchyard by gravediggers in the nineteenth century, which gives us a further indication that it was used as a burial ground from a very early period.

Following the closure of the old Kilgobbin cemetery in 1905, a new burial ground was established close by. One of the most interesting characters interred there is Richard 'Boss' Croker, Tammany Hall politician and horse-trainer.

Croker's finest hour in racing terms came in 1907 when his horse Orby won the Epsom Derby. Orby's win sparked off major celebrations in Ireland – celebratory bonfires blazed in Sandyford and the drink flowed all night long at the Boss's expense. The win, in the back yard of the 'ould enemy', gave a great lift to Irish people everywhere and one Irishwoman was reported to have approached Croker after the race saying, 'Thanks be to Jesus and to you Mr Croker, a Catholic horse has at last won the Derby!'

Such was the excitement caused by the win in Dublin, Croker was awarded the Freedom of the City by the lord mayor a few weeks later. Orby went on to win the Irish Derby and the prestigious Baldoyle Plate and his son Grand Parade won the English Derby in 1919.

Boss Croker made elaborate plans for his own funeral and when he died on 29 April 1922 his body was laid out in evening dress in the chapel on his Glencairn estate. Although the funeral was a private one his coffin was carried by Arthur Griffith, Oliver St John Gogarty and Alfie Byrne, the lord mayor of Dublin. Unusually, Croker had requested a window at the side of his coffin and he had asked that the bones of his famous racehorse Orby be buried beside him. The coffin was placed in a granite mausoleum on the estate.

In 1939 the new owners of Glencairn decided to move Croker's remains to the nearby Kilgobbin cemetery where he was buried alongside his former housekeeper.

Lepers

During the Middle Ages one of the most common and widespread transferable ailments found was the dreaded disease of leprosy. The term 'leprosy' has its origins in the Latin word *liber* which is now taken to mean book. In earlier times, however, *liber* referred to the inner bark of a tree. The name 'libra' subsequently began to be used to describe a range of skin diseases because tree bark had similar peeling qualities to diseased skin. In an Irish context, the word used for leper or leprosy is *lobhar* which is found in the place names of Baile na Lobhar (Leperstown, now Leopardstown) and Tobar na Lobhar (The Leper's Well).

The disease was first recorded 2,500 years ago in India and the theory is that it was brought back to Europe by the armies of Alexander the Great, although it was also known in parts of Africa.

There was huge stigma and fear attached to the disease and lepers were shunned and ostracized. Leprosy was seen as a 'death before death' and priests sometimes performed a death ritual for those afflicted. Sufferers were expected to live in isolation and carry bells or clappers to warn people off. Some churches had what were known as 'squint holes' in their walls so that lepers could observe proceedings at a safe distance from the other worshippers while one church in Pearse Street even had a special 'leper balcony'.

The Anglo-Normans opened leper hospitals all over Ireland during the twelfth and thirteenth centuries and there were several in Dublin. Ailred the Dane, inspired by a hospital he had seen for sick pilgrims in Jerusalem, established the hospital of St John the Baptist just outside the wall of the medieval city of Dublin where Thomas Street now stands. This hospital had a leper hospital attached. In addition to the hospital of St John, there was a hospital for the treatment of lepers in the townland of St Laurence between Chapelizod and Palmerstown.

The Leper Hospital of St Stephen was located close to the site of the old Mercer's Hospital near St Stephen's Green. The owners of the hospital also had a convalescent home at Leopardstown in south Dublin from as early as the year 1230. In that year it was documented that 'the Master and lepers of the house of St Stephen' were given the lands by Geoffrey and Sara Tyrell. This gave rise to the area being called Baile na Lobhar or Lepers Town up until the eighteenth century when it was changed to Leopardstown. Perhaps the name change was instigated by eighteenth century land speculators who realised that the association with leprosy wouldn't have done much for house prices in the area!

One of Dublin's earliest hospitals was built on Lazar's Hill which is now called Townsend Street. The hospital is believed to have been built sometime around 1220 for the use of pilgrims bound for the shrine of St James of Compostella, the patron saint of lepers, in Galicia in northern Spain.

A lazar was another name for a leper and the road leading to the hospital came to be known as Lazar's Hill. The name 'lazar' comes from the Order of St Lazarus, which was formed by monks in the fourth century to set up 'lazar houses' in an effort to combat leprosy.

Over the centuries, the name of the area underwent several transformations and it has been shown in various maps and documents relating to the area as Lazers, Lazie, Lacey, Lowsie and Lousy Hill. Incidentally, the Irish name for Townsend Street is Sráid Cnoic na Lobhair, meaning the Street of the Hill of the Lepers.

Maturin

The author and clergyman Charles Robert Maturin, born in Dublin on 25 September 1782 is best known as the author of the best-selling Gothic classic *Melmoth The Wanderer* published in 1820.

Maturin came from a Dublin Huguenot family. He liked to claim that he was the descendant of Peter Maturin who had been found abandoned on a Paris Street by an aristocratic 'lady of rank'. She apparently gave the child the name of Maturin after the Rue des Mathurins in Paris, the street where the child had been abandoned. Maturin also claimed that Peter later fled to Ireland after serving a lengthy sentence of imprisonment in the Bastille. Several of Peter's descendants were prominent in the established church in Ireland during the eighteenth century and one of these, Charles Maturin's grandfather, Gabriel James, succeeded Jonathan Swift as dean of St Patrick's Cathedral following Swift's death in 1745.

Charles attended Trinity College from where he graduated in 1798 with a classics degree. He was ordained as a minister in the Anglican Church in 1803 and was appointed curate of Loughrea in County Galway where he married Henrietta Kingston before returning to Dublin in 1805 to take up the post of curate at St Peter's parish in Aungier Street.

Maturin began to write in order to supplement his curate's miserable income and his first three novels were published under the pseudonym of Denis Jasper Murphy. He also wrote a number of plays. The most successful of these was *Bertram*, which enjoyed a hugely successful run at the Drury Lane Theatre in 1816, despite receiving a savage review by Samuel Taylor Coleridge.

Maturin's finest hour was the publication of his Gothic masterpiece *Melmoth The Wanderer* in 1820. The novel – said to have been largely written by candlelight in Marsh's library – is a tale of madness, alienation, paranoia and terror and is considered by many to be the definitive Gothic novel.

Maturin and his wife Henrietta bought a large house at 37 York Street just off Stephen's Green with the intention of turning it into a school. The venture was not a success however and they were forced to abandon the project due to their inability to attract a sufficient number of pupils to the school.

Maturin was known to have many unusual habits. One of his York Street neighbours was the poet James Clarence Mangan, who commented on Maturin's peculiar dress sense. Mangan once described seeing Maturin strolling through York Street dressed in an 'extraordinary double-belted and treble-caped rug' with a shoe on one foot and a boot on the other. On other occasions he was to be seen walking through the city wearing a dressing gown and slippers.

While working on his novels, Maturin stuck a red wafer to his forehead as a warning to family and friends that he was not to be disturbed, and he was also known to seal his lips shut with a sticky paste made from flour and water so that he wouldn't be tempted to talk to anyone while he was working.

Maturin loved dancing to such an extent that he even organised morning dancing parties for his friends at his home in York Street. On these occasions he drew all the curtains in the house and lit candles to give an impression of night-time.

Charles Maturin died on 30 October 1824 at the age of forty-two following a short illness. He had suffered periodic bouts of ill health during his last years and it has been said that he died following an accidental drug overdose at his home on York Street.

Newgate Prison

There were two Newgate prisons in Dublin. The original Newgate stood near Cornmarket and Bridge Street, and prior to its use as a prison it had been a watchtower over one of the gates of the old city walls and had been in use since 1285.

The building fell into major disrepair and underwent many renovations during the seventeenth century and in 1773 it was decided to build a new prison across the river at Green Street. Construction was painstakingly slow and the new prison wasn't completed until 1780.

Up until the erection of the new prison, most public hangings in the city had taken place at St Stephen's Green. This necessitated a short cart ride for the condemned man or woman from the old Newgate prison to the gallows on the Green. These processions usually attracted thousands of people and often led to serious civil disorder. With the move to the new prison, it became much easier and safer for the authorities to conduct executions as it meant that they could then hang prisoners within the gaol itself.

The first public hanging to take place at the new Newgate was that of Patrick Lynch, who had been convicted of armed robbery in January 1783. Thousands turned out to view the spectacle and many of the city's streets were blocked for the whole day. Lynch appeared on the balcony at noon and a rope was tied around his neck. The other end of the rope was attached to a new hanging mechanism that was given the following description by the *Dublin Evening Post* : 'a tremendous apparatus for the execution of criminals is fixed at the front of the New Gaol in the Little Green. It consists of a strong iron gibbet with four pulleys of the same metal, underneath which is a hanging scaffold on which the fated wretches are to come out from the centre window, and on a signal the supporters of the scaffold are drawn from under it and the criminals remain suspended.'

Lynch's body was left dangling from the noose for four hours after the execution and his body was then given over to surgeons for dissection.

Newgate was only used as a prison until 1839 but during its sixty-year history there were a high number of escapes and an even greater number of attempted escapes, many of which were undertaken by women prisoners.

Commenting on an attempted mass break-out from Newgate gaol by the women prisoners in September 1787, *Walker's Hibernian Magazine* asserted that 'so astonishing an exertion was never made by a set of females in any gaol in Europe'.

The women had managed to dig a tunnel through the solid foundations of the new prison until it reached a spot on the road outside, directly under a vegetable stall. The tunnel was close to completion when one of their number reported the scheme to the prison authorities, who promptly took action against the would-be escapees.

The building of the tunnel was a remarkable feat and it was said to have been done without the use of tools except for an old poker and a lot of patience. The stones and debris from the tunnel were taken out piece-by-piece and dumped in a large sewerage pit in the prison and the authorities didn't suspect a thing until they were tipped off by the informer. The *Hibernian Journal*, described the women as 'petticoat miners' while the *Freeman's Journal* humorously suggested at the time that King George sent the women 'miners' to help his cousin who was at that time attempting to break through a blockade around the Dutch city of Utrecht.

Almanacs

P.J. McCall (1861–1919), the Dublin newspaper columnist, publican and author of *In The Shadow of St Patrick's*, also spent many years collecting information related to the history of Dublin and Irish almanacs and trade directories.

McCall had originally intended to publish this work in pamphlet form, but for some reason he never quite managed to get round to it. However, the manuscript of McCall's work is still held in the National Library of Ireland and much of the information contained in it was published in 1897 by McCall's friend Edward Evans in a publication entitled *A Historical and Bibliographical Account of Almanacks, Directories, Etc., Published in Ireland From The Sixteenth Century.*

The best known of all the Dublin almanac producers and astrologists was undoubtedly the former cobbler and self-appointed doctor of astrology, fortune-teller and weather forecaster, John Whalley (1653–1724).

One of Whalley's chief rivals in the Dublin almanac industry was Andrew Cumpsty, compiler of the *Dublin Almanack* in 1694 and *A New Almanack* in 1714, printed by Sarah Sadleir in Schoolhouse Lane near High Street.

The *New Almanack* was typical of the almanacs of the day and it contained information such as the high and low tides, position of the moon, fair-days, holy days, swearing days, lists of aldermen, king lists, court-sittings and a complete weather forecast for the entire year.

Disappointingly, Cumpsty declined to make any astrological predictions for that year, presumably on account of the flak that he had received for some of his predictions in preceding years. One disaster that Cumpsty had not foreseen was his own impending death, which took place on 23 November 1713 just as he had applied the finishing touches to what proved to be his last almanac.

Another Dublin quack astrologist named John Coats, author of the *Vox Stellarum,* published in 1714, didn't have any such inhibitions however and he confidently predicted 'great uneasiness' to the king of France in January, 'various sorts of evil effects both on man and beast, and those too of the highest rank as well as those of inferior stations as well as all sorts of fevers, agues and famine in May'. Coats also predicted 'nothing but wars and fighting' for June and July, and nothing but 'craziness, diseases, murder, rapine and general evil for the rest of the year'.

Another Dublin almanac compiler of renown was John Knapp, who first produced Knapp's almanac in 1718. Knapp, a Cork watch and clock mender, was the first Irish astrologer to introduce mathematical tables to Irish almanacs and had an office at the Sign of the Dyal Tavern in Meath Street.

Cumpsty, Coats and Knapp – apart from the fact that they were all astrologers – had one other thing in common: they were all detested by John Whalley and none was spared from the sharpness of his tongue.

Cumpsty often bore the brunt of Whalley's hostility, who once referred to him as a 'Mathe-Maggoty Monster' and a 'Sheep's-faced antagonist' and he also made derisive comments about Coats, whom he referred to as 'the false prophet' and having 'more years than manners'.

Other well-known Dublin almanacs during the eighteenth century were: *The Starry Interpreter, Tom Tatler's Almanack* and *The Cuckold's New Almanack,* published in 1721. These were jointly known as *Swift's Almanacks* and were allegedly printed by Jonathan Swift.

As time wore on the public became increasingly incredulous at these astrologers' rantings and soon all astrological predictions were quietly dropped from the almanacs. However all other features were kept in publications such as *The Gentleman and Citizen's Almanack, The Treble Almanack* and *Hoey's Complete Pocket Companion* and of course the most famous of all almanacs the *Irish Merlin*, better known today as *Old Moore's Almanac*.

Usshers

The Ussher family has had a long-standing connection with Ireland and with Dublin in particular. The evidence of the family's importance to the city can still be seen in some of our existing street and place names such as Ussher's Island and Ussher's Quay and others that have long since disappeared, such as Ussher's Garden, Ussher's Gate, Ussher's Ground and Ussher's Pill.

Ussher's Island takes its name from John Ussher who leased it from the corporation in 1557. The island was said to contain four acres and it was surrounded by the Liffey to the north, two branches of the River Camac to the south and west, and by a pool that came to be known as Ussher's Pill to the east of the Island. The development of Ussher's Quay began at the end of the eighteenth century when the Ussher family decided to build a row of houses on the island.

The Usshers, according to Edward McLysaght's *Irish Families*, were originally a Norman family called Nevill who arrived in Ireland with King John in the early thirteenth century. McLysaght states that one of this family 'took the surname Ussher from the official position he held under that king'. The name itself has its origins in an old French word *uissier* and the Latin *osliarius*, which, roughly translated, means 'doorman' or an official meeter and greeter who keeps out undesirables.

There were several Usshers in Dublin from an early period and one of these was John le Ussher who was constable of Dublin Castle in 1302.

Arland Ussher was mayor of Dublin in 1467. His son Christopher, also served the city in that capacity in 1516 and he held the title of 'Customer and Collector of Dublin' an honour conferred on him by Henry VIII. Christopher's son John was also mayor of Dublin in 1561 and he was described by a contemporary as 'a zealous man in Christ's religion, an honest man of life, and well reported of them that have to do with him'.

Ten years later, John Ussher sponsored the publication of one of the first books written in the Irish language in modern times. The book, published in 1571, was a copy of the Protestant catechism translated into Irish by Sean O'Kearney. Part of the introduction to the book reads: 'Printed in Irish in Atha Cliath (Dublin) at the expense of John Ussher, Alderman, at the head of the Bridge on 20 June 1571.'

One of the most famous Usshers was James Ussher (1581–1656), who served as archbishop of Armagh between 1625 and 1656. Born in the parish of St Nicholas on 4 January 1581, he was a prolific scholar and theologian. Also described as a gifted linguist, Ussher entered Trinity College to study theology at the age of just thirteen.

Ussher's greatest claim to fame was his chronology of creation, published in 1650, that has since become known as the *Ussher – Lightfoot Calendar*. In this work, Ussher came up with a theory that the world actually began on 23 October 4004 BC by counting the number of 'begats' in the Book of Genesis. Later disciples of Ussher's method have even come to the conclusion that the world began at 9 a.m. Greenwich meantime on that date.

Ussher's chronology has been used as a source for the dates in several editions of the King James version of the Bible.

During his lifetime, Ussher compiled a vast collection of books and valuable manuscripts said to number at least 10,000 volumes, and on his death in 1656, the entire collection was donated to Trinity College.

William Mulholland

Dublin man William Mulholland (1855–1935) was instrumental in creating a water supply system for the city of Los Angeles and his monumental achievement has been compared favourably to the building of the Panama Canal.

William Mulholland, son of Dubliners Hugh Mulholland and Ellen Deakers, was born on 11 September 1855 in Belfast while his father, a railway worker was stationed there.

The Mulhollands returned to Dublin in 1860 and put down roots in the north inner city.

William Mulholland attended O'Connell's Christian Brothers School on North Richmond Street. He left before completing his studies there but he was said to have been reasonably well advanced at mathematics. He would later refer to his time at O'Connell's when he was asked about his qualifications to head up one of the largest construction projects ever undertaken. Mulholland replied: 'Well, I went to school in Ireland when I was a boy, learned the three r's and the Ten Commandments – most of them – kissed the Blarney Stone … and here I am.'

Mulholland ran away to sea for the first time when he was fourteen following a row with his father and joined the British merchant navy a year later. After many adventures on the high seas, he ended up working in a logging camp in Michigan where he was almost killed in an accident. While in hospital he overheard doctors saying that they would have to amputate one of his legs that had become infected.

Mulholland decided that he had overstayed his welcome and escaped from the hospital and eventually followed his brother Hugh to Cincinnati, where he arrived almost penniless and suffering from his injuries. He recovered and in 1876 the brothers decided to try their luck in California, walking most of the way to save on the railroad fare. They arrived in San Francisco in February 1877. They travelled south on horseback to Los Angeles, which was then just a small town with less than 10,000 inhabitants.

William got his first job in 1878 with the Los Angeles City Water Company, digging and maintaining water ditches and he studied engineering in the evenings. He rose quickly through the ranks and was appointed superintendent of the company in 1886 at the age of thirty-one. When the city of Los Angeles bought out the company, Mulholland was appointed chief of the Department of Water and Power, a position that he continued to hold until 1928.

By 1900, Los Angeles was expanding rapidly and the city's population had increased to 100,000 and was growing steadily. However, if the city was to expand further, a new water supply was urgently required.

Mulholland soon identified a suitable water source that would sustain the growing city's needs. The only problem was that the source he had in mind – the Owens River – was over 200 miles away from Los Angeles and it belonged to the residents of the Owens Valley.

Mulholland was given the task of building a 233-mile-long aqueduct from the Owens River to the San Fernando Valley but first, all of the land and water rights along the proposed route had to be bought up. This goal was eventually achieved through a combination of legitimate land purchases, bullying and bribery in 1905. Mulholland's massive project took a further eight years to complete and nearly 4,000 workers were employed in the construction of the aqueduct.

As the first waters from the Owens River flowed into the San Fernando reservoir on 5 November 1913, Mulholland made what must surely be one of the shortest speeches ever recorded when he addressed the crowd of 40,000 that had gathered to witness the event. Just as the waters gushed into the reservoir, Mulholland turned to the crowd and simply said: 'There it is. Take it.'

Asculv

The River Steyne or Stein is just one of many Dublin rivers that have been forced underground by the expansion of the city over the course of the centuries. This little river arose somewhere around Harcourt Terrace and made its way to the Liffey via St Stephen's Green, down through Clarendon Street and past the front of Trinity College. It probably entered the Liffey at the junction where Townsend Street and Hawkins Street now stand.

Although it has disappeared from view, the river and the surrounding Stein district featured prominently in the early history of Dublin. The name 'Stein' evolved from the Viking custom of erecting a long stone at their landing places. For centuries this spot was marked by a fourteen-foot-high stone, which only disappeared from public view a little over 200 years ago.

The Stein was one of the city's main landing points during Viking times and it was there that Asculv (or Hasculf) Mac Thorkil landed in 1171 in an attempt to regain control of Dublin, which he had lost to the Anglo-Normans and Dermot McMurrough a year earlier.

In his *Expugnatio Hibernica*, written in the late twelfth century, Giraldus Cambrensis says that McMurrough attacked Dublin on that occasion because he was hell bent on avenging the death of his father, whom the Dublin Hiberno-Norsemen – led by Asculv – had killed and buried at the Thingmote of Dublin along with the corpse of a dog.

McMurrough and the Normans laid siege to the city and Asculv and his men were forced to flee from Dublin in their longboats for the safety of the northern isles. Giraldus claimed in his *Topographia Hiberniae* that Asculv and the fleeing Norsemen attempted to take the famous 'talking crucifix' of Christchurch with them, but no amount of force on their part could get the cross to move.

When Asculv returned to Dublin a year later he was – according to Giraldus – accompanied by reinforcements from the Isle of Man, the Orkney Islands and Norway in a fleet of sixty longboats. Another source from that period – *The Song of Dermot and the Earl* – states that Asculv's fleet consisted of 100 ships containing an attacking force of 20,000 warriors.

Asculv's army landed on the sandy shore of the Steyne and they were led in the attack on Dublin by John 'the Wode', which translates roughly as John 'the mad' or John 'the furious'. Giraldus describes Asculv's forces as: 'warlike figures, clad in mail in every part of their body after the Danish manner. Some wore long coats of mail, others iron plates skilfully knitted together, and they had round red shields protected by iron round the edge.'

They made their way across Hoggen Green and laid siege to the east gate of the city known as St Mary del Dames Gate. John 'the Wode' featured prominently during this attack hacking one Norman's leg off at the hip and killing ten others before being killed himself, either by Walter de Ridelisford or Miles de Cogan, the Norman governor of Dublin.

Many Norsemen were killed in the fighting and Askulv himself was captured while attempting to flee and taken back to the city. Giraldus claimed that de Cogan had originally intended to hold Asculv as a hostage in case of further attacks on the city. Asculv, however, swore that he would return with a larger force to take back what was rightfully his. On hearing this de Cogan ordered Asculv's immediate execution and according to *The Song of Dermot and the Earl* 'they then beheaded Asculv, on account of his outrageous conduct, they rightfully beheaded him on account of his insolence and mad sayings'.

Croke Park

While browsing in a second-hand bookshop recently, I came across a very interesting publication issued by the GAA on Sunday 7 June 1959 to mark the opening of the old Hogan Stand in Croke Park and to celebrate the seventy-fifth anniversary of the association.

The stand was built to replace the old wooden Hogan Stand, which had been erected in 1924 for the first Tailteann Games held in Croke Park, which was a sort of a Gaelic Olympics, if you can imagine such a thing. As well as hurling, football, camogie and handball, there were a wide range of other events such as poetry, Irish dancing, shooting, cycling and swimming. Naturally enough, the swimming competition wasn't held in Croker but it did take place on at least one occasion in the ornamental lake in Dublin Zoo.

The programme informs us that the new Hogan Stand, one of the largest of its kind in Western Europe, could seat 16,000 punters, bringing the total ground capacity to 85,000. The work on the stand was carried out by Thomas McInerney & Sons and it took two years to build using 700 tons of Irish steel reinforcing bars which, the writer helpfully tells us, 'if placed end to end ... would stretch from Dublin to Shannon Airport and back again'.

The booklet also gives a short account of the history and rules and early regulations of the GAA. Teams originally consisted of twenty-one players and 'individual wrestling' was permitted during games – no change there then!

From 1886 to 1910, the scoring area for both hurling and football was larger than it is now. In addition to the H-shaped goalposts used at the moment, there were two additional posts on either side, just like those used in Australian Rules football today. The scoring system was much the same as it is now. A ball going under the crossbar was still worth a goal (three points), while a ball going over the crossbar or anywhere between the outer posts was a point.

The most interesting aspect of this fascinating little publication, however, concerns the history of Croke Park itself. The modern stadium sits on two parcels of land. One of these was a twelve-acre site leased to a John Bradley in 1829, which contained 'an orchard, dwelling house, yard and garden together with the fields adjoining', while the adjoining plot containing twenty-one acres was owned by a Maurice Butterly.

In 1894 a company named the City and Suburban Racecourse and Amusements Grounds bought the land and it was used for a wide variety of sports including Gaelic games, soccer, athletics and whippet racing. The first All-

Ireland finals for hurling and football took place there in 1896.

The grounds were put up for sale in 1906 and two years later Limerick man and GAA member Frank Dineen borrowed heavily and bought the land for £3,250. Dineen didn't buy the land at Jones Road for his own use but he recognised that it would, in time, become an important asset to the GAA.

In 1910 Dineen was forced to sell off a portion of the land to Belvedere College in order to meet his obligations with the bank. The GAA bought the Jones Road sports ground from Dineen in 1913 for £3,500 and renamed it Croke Park in honour of one of its patrons, Dr Thomas Croke.

At that time there were two small wooden stands at the ground on the Hogan Stand side of the ground. One of these was called the 'grand stand' while the structure closer to the canal was called the 'stand'.

Trinity Riots

During the days of British rule in Ireland the arrival of a new lord lieutenant to these shores was traditionally marked by a state procession through the streets of Dublin city and when Archibald William Montgomerie, thirteenth earl of Eglinton was appointed to that position in early 1858, the city prepared to greet him in the traditional fashion.

He arrived at Westland Row railway station on 3 March of that year where he was greeted by the lord mayor and corporation of Dublin and he was escorted with great pomp and ceremony through the streets on his way to Dublin Castle.

At College Green, where the majority of the crowd had gathered to witness the spectacle, a large group of students from Trinity College had assembled just inside the railings and they were heavily armed with a variety of missiles, including stones, eggs, oranges and firecrackers. Although the lord lieutenant was allowed to pass through College Green unmolested, the students indiscriminately pelted everyone else in sight with their missiles.

There was a large detachment of the Dublin Metropolitan Police on duty that day outside the college and they soon became the object of the students' attention. They threw firecrackers and gravel at the police horses and several DMP men had their helmets knocked off during the mêlée. The junior dean of the college, Dr Stubbs, pleaded with the students to withdraw but his pleas fell on deaf ears.

The DMP were under the command of Colonel George Browne – brother of the Dublin poet Felicia Hemans – that day. He was hit in the eye by a missile and the enraged colonel recited the bits of the riot act he could remember and ordered his men to attack the students. The DMP – some on horseback – drew their batons and sabres and charged through the gates of the college trampling the students and using their batons at will.

The students eventually managed to flee to safety inside the college walls, but not before at least thirty of their number were injured. Many received wounds of a serious nature while one student named Leeson was carried in an unconscious state from the scene. The students must have given as good as they got, however, as eighteen DMP men were also injured.

The riot received a great deal of attention in the press and four thousand people signed a petition in the tobacco shop opposite Trinity demanding an inquiry into the behaviour of the police. Questions were asked in relation to the incident in the British House of Lords and House of Commons, and the British government instigated an inquiry into the events some weeks later.

Colonel Browne eventually admitted full responsibility for the incident and he, along with seven of his colleagues, was sent forward for trial at Green Street Courthouse on 21 June 1858.

The DMP gave evidence that they had been severely provoked by the students and one constable claimed that he was forced to draw his sword when one student attempted to cut the reins of his horse. Another stated that while the DMP on horseback had indeed drawn their swords, the students were only hit with the flat side to avoid doing too much damage to them.

The jury retired to consider its verdict and returned just five minutes later with a verdict of 'not guilty' on Colonel Browne, but the damage had been done to his reputation and he resigned from his post as commissioner of police soon afterwards.

Great Fire

During the nineteenth century, two great fires occurred in Dublin city that resulted in major destruction of property and loss of life. The first of these occurred at the Custom House in August 1833 and was described as 'the greatest fire which ever took place in Dublin'; and the second – which sent rivers of flaming whiskey flowing through the streets of the Liberties – took place in June 1875.

The Liberties conflagration began shortly after teatime on Friday 18 June when a fire broke out at Malone's Bonded Spirit Stores in Ardee Street. The blaze was said to have been so intense that the clouds over the city seemed to the thousands of spectators who had gathered to witness the spectacle like a vast red canopy because of the reflection of the flames.

Malone's Bonded Stores contained vast amounts of whiskey and nearly all of the city's leading distilleries such as Jameson's and Power's stored liquors there.

The fire at Malone's took hold very quickly and within a short space of time there were streams of blazing whiskey flowing down Ardee Street. While the city's firemen had arrived immediately after the blaze had started, they were powerless to act because adding water to the burning spirits would only have made matters worse.

Trenches were dug around the surrounding streets and alleyways in an attempt to contain the fiery liquid, but to no avail. Captain Ingram – the first chief officer of Dublin Fire Brigade – ordered his men to erect barricades of sand, tar and rubble at strategic locations to try and halt the flow but the flames rolled over them as if they weren't there. As the fire spread to the nearby streets of Chamber Street, Ormond Street, Cork Street and Mill Street, loud explosions rocked the city as thousands of barrels of whiskey were ignited.

As more and more whiskey stores were set alight the volume of burning whiskey flowing through the streets increased accordingly and, at the height of the blaze, the streets of the Liberties resembled a burning river of flame.

The burning river rapidly made its way down through Cork Street and Ardee Street, consuming several houses in its wake. It continued to flow into Chamber Street and Mill Street, where an entire row of houses was destroyed by the blaze.

Hundreds of residents fled the area in terror from the advancing wall of fire as it consumed everything in its path. Many tenement dwellers lost their homes and their few meagre possessions in the blaze, although none was killed as a direct result of the fire.

However, at least three people died from excessive consumption of alcohol in the immediate aftermath of the fire. According to a report in the *Dublin Evening Post*, some civic-spirited folk remained at the scene of the blaze and 'rescued' some of the barrels of whiskey before the fire could reach them. The Dublin newspapers reported that many of the barrels were taken to other areas of the city where their contents were redistributed in pots, jars, buckets, pitchers and any other container that was handy. There were even reports of men heroically fighting their way through the flames to fill their shoes with whiskey, while some were observed lying face down in the gutter attempting to lick the spirit off the cobblestones.

The fire was eventually brought under control by the erection of large embankments of damp soil at strategic locations in the path of the flames, although it continued to smoulder for several days afterwards.

Bull-baiting

During the eighteenth century in Dublin, the barbaric practice of bull-baiting was a commonplace pastime among the poor of the city. While the gentry and the merchant classes could amuse themselves on the city's bowling greens, promenade around Stephen's Green or indulge in a spot of duelling, the lower orders had to content themselves with a visit to the local cock-pit or the bullring in the city's Cornmarket.

The Cornmarket was one of the main venues for bull-fighting, which took place between bulls and vicious dogs that were specially bred for the purpose. The dogs – similar to today's Staffordshire terriers – were small animals with big heads and had large powerful jaws.

The bull was tied to the bullring with a length of rope just long enough to give him a fighting chance and one or more dogs were then set on the unfortunate animal with the aim of bringing him to the ground. Although the bull usually came off worse in these contests, the dogs were sometimes trampled during the fights and often suffered broken ribs and legs. These dogs were so ferocious that they often fought on despite their injuries and there are tales of dogs continuing to attack the bulls on three legs after a broken leg had been cut off.

At one time it was traditional for every newly elected lord mayor of Dublin to supply the practitioners of bull-baiting with a new rope for their pastime. One mayor who was opposed to the practice refused to supply the rope until the bull-baiters arrived at his house threatening to burn it to the ground, forcing him into a swift change of mind. It is believed that the practice continued until another mayor, who was made of sterner stuff, invited the mob to come and get the rope while pointing a pistol at them. Some hardy souls did have a go but the mayor soon sent them on their way with a few well-aimed blasts of his weapon.

The bulls were usually seized by the bull-baiters on the way to the market or 'borrowed' on their way to the slaughterhouse to provide an afternoon's entertainment for the mob. Although the bull was usually given back to its owner at the end of the fights, they were generally close to death and its market value greatly deflated because of the injuries received.

These bull-fights sometimes led to rioting when the police attempted to intervene, as evidenced by the confrontation that took place in Dublin on St Stephen's Day in 1789 between the bull-baiters and a detachment of soldiers from the Castle guard.

Mr Vance, one of the High Sheriffs of Dublin, was given information that the bull-baiters and their dogs had gathered in a field near North Strand on that day and he rode out with the Castle guard in an attempt to disperse the mob. There was some skirmishing in the field and dogs were set on the sheriff and his men and some stones were thrown. The sheriff ordered his men to fire over the heads of the mob and some arrests were made in the field.

As the crowd made its way back into Abbey Street, the sheriff, for some unknown reason, ordered his men to fire into the crowd, which resulted in the deaths of Farrell Reddy – a Dublin coach maker – and three others.

Vance was later charged in connection with the murder of Farrell Reddy but following an elaborate show trial presided over by Baron Richard Power the jury, after deliberating for only five minutes, found the sheriff not guilty.

The practice of bull-baiting was banned in Ireland in 1798.

Kevin Street Killing

The Dublin newspapers of December 1802 carried details of the trial of William Shields, who had been arrested for the murder of a Dublin cooper, Thomas Ryan, on the night of 14 July earlier that year.

On the night in question Ryan had been in Kevin Street where a bonfire had been lit to celebrate the anniversary of the French Revolution. While the celebrations were in full swing, a number of men armed with shotguns emerged from Cathedral Lane near the fountain on Kevin Street and began to fire into the crowd. Thomas Ryan was fatally wounded in the incident and his body was left lying in Kevin Street until the next morning.

William Shields was later arrested in Navan for the murder of Ryan and he was put on trial for the crime on 6 December 1802. Two other men who had been arrested along with Shields were also charged with the murder but were subsequently discharged.

Richard Roche, a Dublin surgeon, gave evidence to the court that he had examined the deceased and found that he had died from a single shot to the head.

A witness Michael Johnson gave evidence that he knew the accused well and had seen him – with nine or ten others – approach the bonfire near the fountain. Johnson stated that he heard Shields threaten 'to make a lane among the crowd at the fountain' and then heard another man call out to Shields, 'Don't fire, if you do you will commit murder'. A shot rang out immediately afterwards and Johnson saw Ryan fall to the ground.

Another man who had been wounded during the incident, Andrew McManus, gave evidence that there had been a large crowd of men, women and children at the bonfire at the time of the shooting. However, he claimed that he didn't know what the celebration was about, although he did say that the fountain had been covered in green decorations.

Another witness, Margaret Kearns, said that she saw the accused along with three other men named Kinch, Murray and Watson, firing at the crowd that had gathered round the fountain. She then saw Shields firing a single shot at one man, who then slumped to the ground.

Another witness, Michael Reid, with an address at Inns Quay, said that he had met Shields and a guard of soldiers, who were escorting him to Kilmainham Jail. When Reid asked the soldiers what the prisoner had done, Shields interrupted by saying that he had 'only killed a Croppy' and lamented that it wasn't too long in the distant past that he would have been thanked for his actions instead of being arrested.

Witnesses for the defence stated that there was serious rioting taking place in Kevin Street and its environs at the time of the shooting and one witness alleged that he had seen a man brandishing a pistol at one of the bonfires.

One witness – Mr Wilson, who was a magistrate – said that he had prior knowledge that there would be rioting in Kevin Street on the night in question and went to tour the area with a body of watchmen. Wilson claimed that there was also a bonfire in St Patrick's Close and in Patrick Street, where he and his men were stoned by an unruly mob, and that rioting had taken place in the area during the two previous nights.

Despite the overwhelming evidence against Shields, the jury returned after deliberating for half an hour with a 'not guilty' verdict.

First Horse Show

In this day and age the annual Dublin Horse Show attracts a huge number of visitors to the RDS in Ballsbridge and many more follow the proceedings on the television. However, it's a far cry from the very first horse show staged by the Royal Dublin Society on Leinster Lawn in the grounds of Leinster House on 28 July 1868.

Just 6,000 people attended the inaugural event. Horse shows had taken place in 1864 and 1866 but these events – run by the Royal Agricultural Society – were effectively sideshows at their annual agricultural fair. The first of these, organised by Lord Howth, took place on Leinster Lawn on 15 April 1864, and the second took place in September 1866.

In 1867 the Agricultural Society and the Royal Dublin Society – alarmed at the declining number of horses in Ireland – decided to hold a show exclusively for horses and this took place at St Stephen's Green during the month of September that year. This experiment proved so successful that the RDS decided to make it an annual event that has endured to the present day and is a popular feature in Dublin's sporting calendar.

The first horse show run exclusively for horses by the Royal Dublin Society ran for three days beginning on 28 July 1868 in grounds surrounding Leinster House. There was a poor attendance on the opening day – mainly due to heavy rain and the exorbitant admission price of ten shillings – but matters improved greatly over the following two days. The entrance fee was hastily reduced to five shillings and then to two shillings and sixpence, which had the desired effect of increasing the number of visitors.

Nearly 400 horses took part in the show and there were over 6,000 visitors, who were entertained by military bands and a wide variety of sideshows. There were also a wide range of commercial stands in evidence at the first horse show, many of whom were household names in the city.

One of the main attractions of the show was the jumping event which took place in the courtyard of Leinster House on the first day. The event had only been added to the programme three days earlier on the suggestion of Lord Howth, who urged the committee to organise a jumping competition along the same lines as the Islington Horse Show.

The centrepiece of the jumping arena was a stone-wall obstacle described by a writer in the *Irish Farmers Gazette* as being 'five feet ten inches, in cold blood, off wet sawdust, in a crowded courtyard'. So many people had gathered to view the jumping competition that the makeshift wooden terraces collapsed, throwing many spectators into the mud created by the weather. However, there were no reports of any injuries.

The show jumping event was won by a horse called 'Shane Rua' owned by a Mr R. Flynn.

The first Dublin Horse Show was later described by the Irish correspondent of the London *Times* as 'not only the best which has ever been held in Dublin, but in the estimation of some judges it would easily bear comparison with any of the great shows on the other side of the channel'.

In 1881 the Dublin Horse Show moved to its present location at Ballsbridge. At the time that the move was being proposed it was feared in many quarters that Dubliners would not travel to what was then seen as the outskirts of the city for the event. However these fears proved groundless and the Dublin Horse Show continued to grow from strength to strength into the international event that it is today.

Parliament Fire

One Friday evening on 24 February 1792, the old Irish Parliament House on College Green – now owned by the Bank of Ireland – was extensively damaged by fire and it was only saved from total destruction following the intervention of students and staff from Trinity College just across the road.

The Irish Parliament was discussing a bill on 'spirituous liquors' when a shout from above warned the MPs that the building was in flames and in imminent danger of collapse. Instead of immediately fleeing to safety, however, the MPs respectfully waited for the Speaker of the House to officially propose an adjournment, which he did with some haste. Understandably, the motion was unanimously passed without further debate and, with flames leaping all around them, the MPs and members of the public who had been sitting in the gallery, fled in all directions from the advancing inferno.

Within a short space of time the furnishings and fittings of the chamber of the House of Commons had been reduced to ashes, while the great copper dome which covered the round room eventually melted and crashed in on the chamber.

First to arrive at the scene in response to the clanging of the fire bells were the college fire engines manned by students and staff of Trinity College and it was mainly due to their efforts that the fire was contained to the round room of the Parliament building.

The fire was brought under control by nine o'clock that evening and it was entirely extinguished in the early hours of Saturday morning. In the days following the fire, the students – who usually only appeared in newsprint when they had done something wrong – received great praise from all quarters. One newspaper described their efforts as 'almost beyond belief ... amid thousands of idle and unconcerned spectators they alone ... seemed impressed with the importance of preserving an edifice highly ornamental to the capital ... It gives us particular pleasure to be able to announce the strenuous efforts of these gentlemen'.

The students had been barred from sitting in the public gallery of the House of Commons some time earlier, but despite their 'strenuous efforts' to save the building, they still weren't allowed to sit there afterwards because of objections made by several MPs.

In the immediate aftermath of the fire several possible temporary locations for the sitting of Parliament were proposed, such as Trinity College, the Rotunda and Leinster House. It was eventually decided that Parliament would sit at the Blue Coat Hospital in Phoenix Park and that the Commons would take up temporary residence in the Records Office in Dublin Castle while the parliament building was being repaired.

A few days after the fire a committee was appointed to establish the cause of the blaze. Although many theories were advanced as to the cause of the inferno it was eventually established that the department responsible for the maintenance of the building had been experimenting with a new heating system which conveyed hot air from a furnace around the walls of building. One of the pipes just under the roof had ruptured and sparks from the furnace had apparently set the woodwork on fire with disastrous consequences.

The Parliament building was eventually restored at a cost of approximately £50,000 and it was sold to the Bank of Ireland following the Act of Union of 1800.

Father Vlad

An unusual trial took place at Green Street Court on 7 December 1855 when Father Vladimir Petcherine, a Redemptorist priest from Kingstown (Dun Laoghaire) was accused of burning a Protestant bible 'in company with books acknowledged to be of an improper and immoral character' and a number of other books at the parish church in Kingstown.

Earlier in October that year Father Petcherine had mounted a campaign in Kingstown against 'immoral literature' and he urged his parishioners to hand in books, newspapers and periodicals which might be seen as being offensive to one's morals.

A large number of these items were handed over and on 5 November, Father Petcherine gathered them all into two wheelbarrows and brought them to the parish church where they were set on fire in the yard.

Reverend Robert Wallace, the Protestant rector of Kingstown, was passing the church some time afterwards and he noticed some boys kicking the smouldering remains of books, one of which he discovered was the remains of a bible.

Four days later he got up in front of his congregation and spoke at length on the subject of bible burning. He also wrote a pamphlet on the issue and letters to the newspapers in connection with the matter.

The authorities took an interest in the case at this point and Father Petcherine was subsequently charged with the crime of 'blasphemously burning and treating with contempt the Holy Scriptures, thereby tending to bring religion into contempt at Kingstown on November 5th inst'.

The case created a huge amount of public interest in Dublin and when Petcherine's trial opened on the morning of 7 December, the area surrounding the courthouse was thronged with curious onlookers. Admission to the courthouse was by ticket only and by the time the judges arrived the court was full to capacity.

The attorney-general, stating the case for the prosecution, said that if Father Petcherine had only burnt books of an immoral nature then he would have no case to answer but if it was proven that he had burnt copies of the 'sacred writings' along with them then the priest would be seen to have carried religious zeal' beyond its legitimate and justifiable bounds. He also stated that the evidence would show that the latter was in fact the case.

Christopher Duff, one of the boys who had witnessed the fire, said in evidence that he had been at Father Petcherine's house on 5 November and had seen a copy of the New Testament being loaded into the wheelbarrow along with the other books.

Four other witnesses for the Crown, including a Kings-town magistrate, gave evidence that they had seen Protestant versions of the bible in Fr Petcherine's wheelbarrows. Despite the evidence however, Petcherine was found 'not guilty' and when he emerged from the courthouse he was met by a huge crowd that had gathered to support him. Cheering erupted, hats were thrown in the air and it took the priest a long time to make his way to his carriage through the crowd who had pressed forward to shake his hand.

So great was the public interest in the case that many newspapers covering the trial in the city sold out in record time that evening. It was also reported that a large number of houses in the vicinity of the courthouse were illuminated by torchlight to celebrate the acquittal of the priest, while another bemused correspondent said that 'the exultation of the lower orders at the result of the trial beggars all powers of description'.

Three days later, Edward Hayden, described as a supporter of Father Petcherine, was found guilty of the aggravated assault of one of the Crown's witnesses in the case and was sentenced to serve three months imprisonment with hard labour.

John Atherton

In December 1640, John Atherton, bishop of Waterford, was tried and convicted for engaging in the act of sodomy with his steward and tithe proctor John Childe, for which he was subsequently hanged on Gallows Green in Dublin. There were several lurid accounts written about the case afterwards including one pamphlet which falsely claimed that the bishop had been charged with bestiality and 'uncleanness with a cow and other creatures'. Another contemporary publication made the claim that he had been convicted for 'incest, buggery and many other enormous crimes'.

John Atherton was born in Somerset, England, in 1598. He was a member of a wealthy English family and he received his education at Oxford University. Shortly after leaving Oxford he became a rector in the Church of England and he served as prebendary of St John's in Dublin and chancellor of Christchurch. He came to the attention of Thomas Wentworth, earl of Strafford and lord lieutenant of Ireland, who appointed him bishop of Waterford in 1636.

In 1640 he was accused of engaging in an act of sodomy with John Childe, a charge that he strongly denied in court. However, Childe gave evidence against him and the bishop was condemned to death. It is ironic that Atherton was one of the first men to receive the death sentence for the crime of sodomy, as he had been a leading advocate in the campaign to make the act of sodomy punishable by death.

The bishop was condemned to death on Friday 27 November and was taken to Dublin Castle to await execution. Although Atherton had pleaded not guilty to the charge in court he decided that the sanctity of the churchyard would be too good for his remains and he summoned the clerk of St John's Church and the verger of Christchurch to ask them to bury him under a rubbish heap in the furthermost corner of St John's churchyard just off Fishamble Street. Full of remorse, Atherton attributed his downfall to the 'reading of bad books, viewing of immodest pictures, frequenting of plays and drunkenness etc.'. He also decided at one point that 'a dog's death was too good for him' and considered asking to be beheaded instead of hanged.

On the morning of his execution, Atherton was taken in a coach to the gallows, which was then located close to where Parkgate Street is now. He was escorted by two city sheriffs and the county sheriff 'with a great company of halberds (swordsmen) to assist him'. As the grim procession made its way past Christchurch, the 'passing-bell' was tolled. One eyewitness, Nicholas Bernard, dean of Ardagh, said that he had never seen either the town or the castle so crowded before.

When he had completed his last speech at the foot of the gallows, Bishop Atherton climbed the ladder and placed his head in the noose. His hands were untied and he was allowed to fasten a handkerchief over his face. He turned to the hangman saying 'honest friend, when thou art ready tell me, and I will tell thee when I am ready' and he handed him the customary fee that was paid to ensure a quick execution.

He was left hanging for nearly an hour after which his corpse was taken back across the Liffey in a coach and later that night he was buried in the spot that he had requested in St John's churchyard.

Atherton's steward, John Childe, was executed shortly afterwards on the bridge of Bandon in County Cork.

James Annesley

Anglesea Street in the heart of Dublin's Temple Bar takes its name from Arthur Annesley, earl of Anglesea, who held several leases on properties there during the middle of the seventeenth century.

In 1743, a curious case involving James Annesley, great grandson of Arthur, took place in the High Court in Dublin. James was a son of Arthur Annesley, who held the title of Lord Altham, and Mary Sheffield, daughter of the duke of Buckingham.

James was born in Wexford in 1715 and his parents separated in February of the following year. His mother returned to England where she died some years later. James continued to live with his father and a few years later they moved to a house at Cross Lane in Dublin along with his father's mistress, a Miss Gregory.

The new Lady Altham wasn't too fond of young James and in 1724 when he was only eight years old she persuaded his father to send him to live at a lodging house, which was either in Fleet Street or Ship Street. He was educated at Barnaby Dunn's school in Werburgh Street.

James was later sent to live at the home of a dancing master named Cavanaugh, who was instructed to keep the boy out of the way. However, James didn't like it there and escaped soon afterwards. He knew that he couldn't go home because of Miss Gregory's opposition to him and he became a homeless vagrant, living on his wits in the back alleys and laneways of Dublin.

James was eventually taken into the care of John Purcell, a butcher in the Ormond Market who had been introduced to the boy by Dominic Farrell, a Dublin linen merchant.

Farrell went to see Lord Altham to plead with him to take responsibility for his son, but Altham apparently washed his hands of any responsibility towards the child, claiming that Miss Gregory wouldn't allow him inside the house.

James continued to live with Purcell and his wife at their home in Phoenix Street until the death of Lord Altham in 1727. In the normal run of things, young James Annesley should have been the next Lord Altham, but his father's brother Richard had other ideas. Not too many people knew of James' existence and Richard wanted the title for himself.

Richard decided to get rid of the youngster and he had James arrested in 1728 on a trumped-up charge of having stolen some silver. The boy – who was still only twelve years old – was taken to Ringsend, where he was put on board a transport ship bound for Philadelphia. There he was immediately sold into slavery on the instructions of his uncle.

Following a series of adventures in America he eventually escaped to Jamaica in 1740. He arrived back in Dublin two years later along with a wealthy companion Daniel McKircher, who was determined to help him regain his estate and title.

Uncle Richard, however, wasn't about to give up the title easily and he attempted to have his nephew killed on several occasions. Once, at the Curragh, Richard's son Francis and one of his servants attempted to kidnap James but they were foiled by James' companions, who gave them a 'sound horsewhipping' to the great pleasure of the race-goers.

James eventually instigated proceedings against his uncle in the High Court on 11 November 1743 and after a trial that lasted fifteen days the jury found in the younger Annesley's favour.

However, Richard appealed against the decision and the case dragged on for an incredible sixteen years until 1759 when James died suddenly at the age of forty-three. Richard died two years later and the estate eventually passed into the hands of his son Arthur.

Soup Kitchens

Although Dublin was not as badly affected as other parts of Ireland during the Great Famine, which began in 1845, many starving people flooded into the city in search of food. One of the easiest ways to feed the starving masses was through the use of soup kitchens, which were capable of feeding thousands on a daily basis.

One of the best-known soup kitchens in Dublin was at Croppies Acre in front of the Royal Barracks (Collins Barracks), which was set up by the famous French chef Alexis Soyer. Soyer was born at Meaux-on-Brie on the Marne in 1810 and he served his time as a chef at some of the best restaurants in France. He moved to England during the 1830s. There he established himself as one of the finest chefs in the country and in 1837 he was appointed head chef of the Reform Club.

It was while he was working at the Reform Club that Soyer became interested in the plight of the victims of the great Irish famine. In 1847, Soyer wrote several letters to the press on the subject and in April of that year he was appointed by the British government to open a soup kitchen in Dublin from which he dispensed meals at half the usual cost to the British Exchequer.

While in Ireland, Soyer produced a booklet entitled *Soyer's Charitable Cookery or the Poor Man's Regulator* which he dedicated 'for the benefit of the working, labouring and poorer classes of Ireland and Britain'. The booklet, aimed primarily at the upper classes, appealed for increased charitable funding for the victims of the Irish famine and gave details of how to set up a soup kitchen. It also contained several recipes for cheap and nourishing meals such as, 'meagre pea soup, curry fish, cheese stirabout, St Patrick's soup, and oyster porridge'.

Soyer was invited to come to Dublin by the British government in the spring of 1847 to set up a soup kitchen. His kitchen supplied an estimated one million meals in the space of five months – an average of 8,750 per day. Soyer claimed that one bowl of his soup, when taken with some bread or a biscuit, provided enough nourishment to keep a healthy man going for a whole day. Soyer further claimed that his soup had been given the seal of approval by 'numerous noblemen, members of Parliament and several ladies'. The soup was made from leg of beef, water, onions, flour, pearl barley, dripping, salt and brown sugar.

Soyer's soup wasn't universally welcomed, however, and there were some complaints that it actually harmed a number of people who had been suffering from dysentery.

The soup kitchen itself was described in Cecil Woodham-Smith's book *The Great Hunger* as 'a wooden building, about forty feet long and thirty feet wide, with a door at each end; in the centre was a 300-gallon soup boiler, and a hundred bowls, to which spoons were attached by chains …'

People were admitted to the hall in shifts of 100 at a time by the ringing of a bell. When they had finished the soup, they were handed a piece of bread and left by the second door. The bowls were then cleaned and the next batch of people were summoned, again by the ringing of the bell.

Loughlinstown Camp

During the turmoil and political upheaval that preceded the 1798 rebellion, one of the events that the British government feared the most was a French invasion of Ireland and there was particular concern that this invasion would most likely take place in Dublin.

In 1794 a British army officer, Colonel George Napier, pinpointed Killiney Bay as the most likely spot for such an invasion and he proposed the erection of a large military camp at Loughlinstown in order to defend the city from any such attack. Napier specifically chose Loughlinstown because it was on a height overlooking Killiney Bay but was yet far enough away to be out of range of the French artillery.

The British government agreed with Napier's assessment of the situation and a 120-acre site in the townland of

Lehaunstown on the Loughlinstown estate was purchased. A camp capable of holding up to 5,000 soldiers was established there by mid-1795.

The garrison of 4,000 men was initially billeted in tents on the site but a drawing in John Ferrar's *A view of ancient and modern Dublin* of the camp in 1796 reveals that the vast majority of the soldiers were by then accommodated in rows of wooden huts. Ferrar said that there were sixty-four of these wooden huts, each one with accommodation for thirty-six soldiers and two NCOs, and there were another sixty-five assorted wooden buildings including officers' quarters, kitchens and mess-houses.

Fears of an invasion were heightened in December 1796 when a French landing at Bantry Bay was stymied only by bad weather conditions. In response, the British government appointed Major La Chausse – a Frenchman serving in the British Army – to further strengthen the fortifications at Killiney.

La Chausse conducted a survey of the bay and made several recommendations for its defence including the placing of big guns on the cliffs overlooking the shore at Killiney and that all 'hedges, ditches and ravines' in the vicinity should be cut back so as not to give the enemy cover.

Despite the elaborate precautions, the expected French invasion never materialised and Loughlinstown camp was closed down in 1799 without seeing any action. During its short existence, stories written in the Dublin press in relation to the camp were mainly concerned with the leisure time activities of its inhabitants.

Loughlinstown was more like a holiday camp than a military installation and on weekends during the summer months, the roads to the camp were filled with daytrippers anxious to view, as one writer in the *Freeman's Journal* put it, 'the martial splendour of the tented field'.

The writer described the scene on the Bray Road on Sundays as 'a scene of the true grotesque and highly ludicrous' and said that 'every vehicle from the Royal George to the dust cart was in motion on the Bray road, and every hack horse, mule, or ass that could be procured for hire, joined in the cavalcade'.

Visitors to the camp were entertained by marching military bands during the daytime and at night there was music and dancing in the purpose-built Assembly Rooms. Meals and refreshments were also on sale and there was a coffee room and several dining and beer tents at the camp.

Very little of military significance ever took place at Loughlinstown Camp, but in 1798 John and Henry Sheares, two brothers, both leading members of the United Irishmen, were charged with high treason and accused of formulating a plan to attack and take over the camp. Both were executed in July of that year.

The camp was broken up in April 1799 and the site was divided and sold off as farmland in 1812.

John O'Keeffe

John O'Keeffe, the writer and playwright, was born at Abbey Street, Dublin, on 24 June 1747. He was educated by the Jesuits as a child and he later studied art at the Royal Academy in Shaw's Court off Dame Street, with his brother Daniel, under the guidance of Robert West. He spent a few years working as an artist in London where, as he said himself, 'I was afraid of opening my lips, lest I should be laughed at for my Dublin brogue'.

He joined the Smock Alley Theatre in 1764 as an actor and he travelled the country in this capacity for the next ten years. He also began his career as a playwright around this time and his first contribution was a five-act comedy entitled *The Generous Lovers*.

O'Keefe was married to the well-known Cork-born actress Mary Heaphy (1757–1813), daughter of Tottenham Heaphy, who managed theatres in Cork and Limerick. They married in 1774 and appeared together in productions at the Smock Alley and Crow Street theatres. Because of the fact that O'Keeffe was a Catholic and Heaphy a Protestant, two separate wedding ceremonies had to be performed in order to keep both families happy. The marriage didn't last for very long and sometime around 1780 Mary became involved in another relationship with an actor called George Graham.

When O'Keeffe found out about the relationship he was said to have beaten Mary so ferociously that he 'demolished his wife's nose' according to the writer of a biographical sketch of O'Keeffe in the *Catalogue of Five Hundred*

Celebrated Authors, published in 1788. The couple had three children: John Tottenham, Adelaide and Gerald. Following the break-up of his marriage, O'Keeffe left for England, bringing his children with him. According to his daughter Adelaide, O'Keeffe never mentioned his wife's name again and when Gerald died in 1787 he became reclusive and withdrawn.

He was also nearly blind at that stage, having suffered for some years from a serious inflammation of the eyes, which he sustained when he fell drunk into the river Liffey at Ringsend one dark December night. O'Keeffe compounded the problem by seeking remedies from quacks – including electric shock treatment – which ultimately led to him losing his sight. O'Keeffe spent his last years living in a cottage in Southampton where he died on 4 February 1833.

Although he is chiefly remembered for his plays and other dramatic works, O'Keeffe also left behind his memoirs, *Recollections of the Life Of John O'Keeffe* which he dictated to his daughter Adelaide during the latter years of his life. His memoirs contain many witty and amusing anecdotes of life in Dublin and paint a fascinating picture of the city's characters and the personalities of the late eighteenth and early nineteenth centuries.

O'Keeffe was on first name terms with all of Dublin's leading actors and playwrights, and his book contains many references to theatrical luminaries, such as Peg Woffington, Spranger Barry, Richard Brinsley Sheridan, Henry Mossop, David Garrick and others. Other well-known Dublin characters such as Jonathan Swift, George Faulkner, the Dublin printer, and the informer Leonard McNally are mentioned, but there are also many other tales related to duelling, drinking and forgotten Dublin pastimes and customs.

O'Keefe also recounts several amusing tales of some of the city's characters, such as Travair, the cobbler, and the eccentric Captain Debrisay, who are not generally mentioned in other contemporary works.

Oxmanstown

On the north shore of the River Liffey the modern district of Oxmantown represents an area settled by the Hiberno-Norse community of Dublin following the arrival of the Anglo-Normans in the late twelfth century. The area was originally known under the variants of Ostman's Town, Houstmanebi, Ostmanby, Oustmanton and Oestmantown. All of these variations in spelling refer to the 'men who came from the east', i.e. the Vikings. There may have been an earlier Hiberno-Norse Viking settlement in the area as the church of St Michan had been established there some eighty years earlier.

The exact location of the settlement is hard to define but it seems to have been located roughly in the area stretching from the Liffey up as far as King Street, by Arbour Hill to the west and St Michan's on the east side. The famous green or Common of Oxmantown was located in and around the Smithfield market area. The green was used for many years as a pasture for cattle and sheep and also as a place of recreation for the citizens of Dublin. The Green was eventually covered over after the corporation decided to sell it off in lots for building purposes in 1664.

In his contribution to *Holinshed's Chronicles*, written in 1577, Richard Stanihurst makes several references to the 'Faire-Greene of Ostmonstowne', which he says was covered in trees in the twelfth century. According to Stanihurst, timber from Oxmantown was exported to England by the English King, William Rufus, to be used in the construction of the roof at Westminster Hall 'where', Stanihurst intriguingly adds, 'no English Spider webbeth or breedeth to this day'.

Stanihurst also alludes to a resident of Oxmantown who lived, not on the green, but under it. Stanihurst was referring to a famous Dublin thief called Scaldbrother who lived in a cave known as 'Scaldbrother's Hole', which was said to stretch a long distance under Oxmantown Green.

Scaldbrother was said to have been so confident in his ability to outrun all pursuers that he would often wait for them under the gallows at 'Gybbett Slade' near Arbour Hill before disappearing into his lair with his booty. Scaldbrother's luck eventually ran out and he was hanged on the gallows at Gybbet Slade. This area has been identified in other sources as Gibbet's Glade and Gibbet's Shade.

Scaldbrother's Hole is mentioned again in Nathaniel Burton's *Oxmantown and its Environs* written in 1845. Burton says that builders digging foundations for houses at Oxmantown regularly broke through into the cave while some Smithfield brewers used part of the thief's lair for the storage of beer.

There is another Oxmantown legend concerning Little John, partner-in-crime of the English outlaw Robin Hood. The story goes that following the death of Robin Hood, Little John went on the run from the forces of the law and made his way to Dublin. During his time here he was said to have impressed the natives with his archery skills and he once fired an arrow from the Old Bridge of Dublin all the way to Arbour Hill. The place where the arrow landed was allegedly known for some years afterwards as 'Little John his Shot'.

There is another variation of this legend, which states that Little John fired his arrow into a mound of earth in St Michan's churchyard known as 'the Giant's Grave'. Like ScaldBrother, Little John is said to have met his end at the end of a rope at Gibbet's Shade.

Grafton Street

Dublin's premier shopping thoroughfare Grafton Street, recently described as one of the world's most expensive places to rent retail property, was partially laid out during the late seventeenth century and it was originally called 'the highway to St Stephen's Green'. Before it was developed, the southern portion of the street was used for the cultivation of wheat and it was known as Crosse's Garden.

Grafton Street underwent further development at the beginning of 1712 when the Dublin corporation allocated funds for 'making a crown causeway' through the street. It was initially developed as a residential street and during the eighteenth century many well-known Dubliners lived there. Louis Du Val, manager of the Smock Alley Theatre, lived there in 1733, as did the family of famous Gothic novelist Charles Robert Maturin.

With the opening of Carlisle Bridge (O'Connell Bridge) in 1792, Grafton Street gradually began to change to a centre of commercial activity and many of the houses were converted into shops. There were several taverns on the street including the Black Lyon and the City Tavern as well as a number of lottery offices, booksellers and private schools.

The street was given its current name after either Henry Fitzroy, first duke of Grafton, or his son Charles Fitzroy, second duke of Grafton and lord lieutenant of Ireland, who was once described by Jonathan Swift as a 'slobberer without one good quality'.

The first duke of Grafton, Henry Fitzroy, is described in the *Dictionary of National Biography* as 'the most popular and ablest of the sons of Charles II … with a strong and decided character, reckless daring and a rough, but honest temperament'. He was given the title of duke of Grafton in 1675. The duke had once been a staunch ally of James II but was one of the first to abandon him when William of Orange landed in Ireland in 1688. He was mortally wounded at the siege of Cork and died on 9 October 1690.

However, it seems more likely that the street was named after his son Charles, second duke of Grafton and lord lieutenant of Ireland from 1721 to 1724. Regarded by his peers as a dandy and a spendthrift, the duke had wildly extravagant tastes.

Grafton, who was also said to be extremely fond of 'drinking and wenching', displayed little interest in the world around him and he viewed those who discussed 'depressing topics' such as poverty or the education and health of the poorer classes as 'unhealthy cranks, wild men, or perhaps even republicans'.

In 1706 he called for tougher measures against Irish Catholics and some years later gave his wholehearted support to a bill put before the Irish Parliament which proposed to banish all Catholic priests from Ireland on pain of castration if they refused.

Most commentators of his time had little regard for the duke, his business acumen or political abilities and many saw him as a downright liability. In his memoirs, Lord Waldegrave said that Grafton was a man who 'usually turned politics into ridicule, had never applied himself to business, and as to books was totally illiterate', while Horace Walpole described him as 'a fair weather pilot that knew not what he had to do when the first storm arose'.

The second duke of Grafton died after falling from his horse while hunting at the age of seventy.

Red Lighthouse

The distinctive red lighthouse at the end of the Great South Wall at Ringsend is one of the most familiar landmarks in Dublin Bay. Officially known as the Poolbeg Lighthouse, it has appeared as a backdrop to many films, documentaries and television adverts. In the distant past, this area was known as Poll Beag meaning 'little pool' and it was – before the development of Dublin port – the main anchorage for shipping arriving in Dublin.

The current lighthouse has acted as a beacon for mariners since 1820. This replaced another lighthouse built in 1767 but even before that there were floating lights in some shape or form on the same site.

In 1731 the corporation of Dublin gave the Ballast Board the go-ahead to erect a floating light at the end of the south wall or 'the piles' as it was then known. However, another four years passed before the board was able to report that it was in a position to install a floating light to be built on the same design as a light ship at the Nore in England. At the close of 1735 the Ballast Board reported that 'a great many masters of ships' had met to approve the plan and all were in agreement that 'such a floating light would be of great service for ships, for they then would be able to come into Polebegg in the darkest night ...'

The floating light – which burned coal fires in braziers by night and displayed a flag by day – was in place in early 1736 and it was manned around the clock by two hands at eighteen pounds and sixteen pounds per annum and 'two lusty boys' who were each paid ten pounds per annum. The manager of the lightship was James Palmer and it was known as 'Palmer's Lightship' or the 'Dublin Lightship'.

By 1761 the floating lightship was in a bad state of repair and costing so much money to keep afloat that the Ballast Office decided to build a permanent lighthouse at 'the end of the piles'.

An engineer named John Smith was asked to design and build the lighthouse and his first task was to construct foundations that could withstand the power of the Irish Sea. He achieved this by enclosing large stones in huge wooden casings and sinking them. Work on the lighthouse, a conical structure surrounded by an iron balcony and spiral staircase, was completed by June 1767. *Exshaw's Magazine* described the new lighthouse as 'a work of the highest utility, tending to the prosperity and increase of commerce, and to the preservation of her hardy sons, who lead her through every clime'.

It was originally called the George Lighthouse and was officially opened on 29 September 1767. It was the first lighthouse in the world to use candles instead of coals to provide light, and twenty years later the Poolbeg Lighthouse attained another first when it became the first lighthouse to use spermaceti oil lamps.

In 1768 Smith was thanked by the city assembly for his efforts and was awarded a piece of silver plate and twenty guineas. Local tradition says that his wife should have been given the prize, as it was she who had suggested the sinking of the wooden casings loaded with stones. The George Lighthouse remained in use until it was replaced in 1819–20 by the present structure designed by George Halpin, Inspector of Lighthouses. The Poolbeg Lighthouse had a live-in lighthouse keeper until December 1968 and it went automatic on New Year's Day in 1969.

Fyan's Castle

No one can say with any degree of certainty when exactly Dublin became a walled town, but it is known that the city was defended by a wall fortified by at least twenty towers and defended by gates.

One such tower was Fyan's or Fian's Tower, which was also known as Proudfoote's Castle. The tower – located on Wood Quay at the bottom of Fishamble Street – was first mentioned in 1456 when it was leased to John Marcus for a term of thirty years at a rent of six pence per year. At that time it was described simply as 'the tower over the fish slip'. The tower was described in a report written for lord deputy of Ireland, John Perrot, in 1585 as: 'Mr Fian's Castell ... a square towre, fowre storie hie, 38 foot sqware one way and 20 foote another way, towe [two] spickes or lowpes [defensive slits] in the loer storie and windows in every of the other rowmes, the wall fowre foote thicke and 42 foote hie, and the grounde firme 8 foote hie from the channell within the castell.'

The tower was named after the Fyan family who first occupied it during the fifteenth century. In his book on Irish surnames, *More Irish Families*, Edward McLysaght states that the now extremely rare surname of Fyan was first recorded in Dublin during the fifteenth century. Father Patrick Woulfe in his *Irish Names and Surnames* says that Fyan is a variant of Fagan which is derived from the Latin *paganus*, meaning the 'pagan' or the 'rustic'.

The Fyans were an eminent Dublin merchant family during the Middle Ages and they figure prominently in the municipal records for the city from as early on as the fifteenth century. Gilbert's *Calendar of Ancient Records of Dublin* records that several members of the Fyan family held high office in the city throughout the ages. John Fyan was mayor of Dublin in 1472 and 1479, while his descendant Richard Fyan held the same office in 1549 and 1564. Another family member, Thomas Fyan, was sheriff of Dublin in 1540.

In 1623, it was recorded that one Alderman Fyan, a member of Dublin city council, was named, along with several other prominent citizens, as one who had given aid and shelter to several 'Jesuits, Friars and Popish priests' who had come to Dublin for a religious conference. As a consequence, the Council of Ireland issued a proclamation ordering all such persons to leave the city within forty days.

In 1550 one Richard Fyan described as a 'merchant of the city of Dublin' and a former mayor of Dublin made an application to the English Privy Council for permission to build 'six looms of linen and woollen yarn' on the site of the former nunnery of St Mary of Hogges, which, Fyan said, would give employment 'to a great number of persons now idle'.

The Barry family, who later became lords of Santry, owned Fyan's Castle from 1614 until about 1660, when they sold it to a tanner named Francis Sleigh, who in turn sold it on to Philip Carpenter just three years later. Carpenter had the castle fitted out for use as a prison and in 1666 the Dominican priest, Father John O'Hart, was incarcerated there along with two other members of the order.

For a great part of the seventeenth century Fyan's Castle was known as Proudfoot's Castle. Although its not clear if he ever owned it, Richard Proudfoot reclaimed land in the immediate vicinity of the castle and developed it between the years of 1605 and 1607.

The castle seems to have been intact until the middle of the nineteenth century and its foundations were uncovered during road works in 1974.

Thomas Crawley

On the night of 17 February 1802, police were called to a lodging house at 9 Peter's Row in Dublin. When the police entered the building they discovered the bodies of two women, Catherine Davidson – proprietor of the lodging house – and her maid Mary Mooney. Both had been bludgeoned to death.

Eight days later, an apprentice solicitor named Thomas Radcliffe Crawley – a lodger at the house – was arrested in Newry in connection with the double murder and taken back to Dublin to face trial.

The trial, presided over by the infamous 'hanging judge', Lord Norbury, began on 1 March at Green Street Courthouse, where Crawley was accused of causing the deaths of the two women by hitting them repeatedly over the head with a hammer. Crawley, who had no previous convictions, was an apprentice attorney and also held a commission in the Roscommon militia for a period.

FRANK HOPKINS

At his trial, which created huge public interest, Crawley
was defended by the well-known lawyers John Philpot
Curran and Leonard McNally. Crawley was brought to the
courthouse in heavy chains and McNally immediately asked
the judge to have them removed. A blacksmith was called in
to remove the heavy manacles, but he was unable to remove
them within a reasonable amount of time so Crawley was
forced to wear them in the dock for the duration of the
trial.

Curran tried to have the trial postponed on the grounds
that there had been so much 'public excitement' in relation to
the case that it would be impossible to bring witnesses for the
defendant into court because their lives would be at risk.

However, Curran's objections were quickly dismissed
and the trial went ahead. The first witnesses called were
physician Henry Roe and Joseph, a surgeon. Both men had
examined the bodies of the two women on the night of the
murders and both were in agreement that they had died
from wounds inflicted with a heavy iron instrument.

Next to give evidence on behalf of the prosecution was
John McCullough, a cobbler who lived at Bow Lane close
to the scene of the murders. McCullough stated that some
time between six and seven on the night of 17 February,
Crawley had come into his workshop and asked him for the
loan of a hammer to fix some shelves. McCullough said that
he was using his own hammer at the time but gave him the
loan of a coal hammer instead. The hammer was produced
in court as evidence and McCullough's son William verified
that it was the same one that Crawley had returned to him
later that same evening.

Another witness, clergyman Joseph Elwood, who also lived at the lodging house on Peter's Row, gave evidence that Crawley – who had only moved into the house four weeks earlier – had asked him if Mrs Davidson had kept any money on the premises and had also questioned him as to his own financial state.

Elwood told the court that on the night of the crime he heard 'violent shrieks and moans' coming from downstairs but said he didn't do anything about it because he had often heard Mrs Davidson quarrelling with her maid. About an hour after the shouting had stopped Elwood said that he met the highly agitated Crawley, who asked him for a drink and a loan of some money. He found the bodies of Catherine Davidson and her maid in the parlour soon afterwards.

After listening to all of the evidence, the jury was sent out to consider its verdict and returned to pronounce Crawley guilty after an absence of only ten minutes. Norbury donned the black cap and sentenced him to death and Crawley was hanged in front of Newgate prison on 12 March 1802.

Olympics

When the Dublin Fine Gael TD and MEP Gay Mitchell proposed holding the Olympic Games in Dublin some years ago, he wasn't the first politician to make such a suggestion. In early February 1933, the first commissioner of the Garda Síochána and leader of the Blueshirts, General Eoin

O'Duffy, floated the idea of staging the Olympic Games in the Phoenix Park.

O'Duffy was deeply involved in Irish sporting organisations at the time. He was head of the NACA (National Athletic and Cycling Association of Ireland) and was president of the Irish Olympic Council. O'Duffy was involved in sending an Irish team to the Amsterdam Olympics in 1928 where Pat O'Callaghan won the first of his two medals and he helped secure government funding to send a four-man Irish team to the 1932 Olympic Games in Los Angeles.

Ireland won two gold medals at the Los Angeles games and one of the winners, Bob Tisdall only got onto the team after writing a letter to O'Duffy early in 1932 asking to be allowed represent Ireland in the 400 metres hurdles even though he had never actually competed in the event before.

In a series of interviews given to the national newspapers in February 1933, O'Duffy suggested that Ireland should apply to the Olympic Council for the right to stage the 1940 Olympic Games in the Phoenix Park.

O'Duffy claimed to have approached the president of the Olympic Council, Count de Baillet-Latour, with his idea and he was 'agreeably surprised to find that the suggestion was well received'. O'Duffy based his optimism on the grounds that Ireland had done well in the 1932 Olympics and the fact that over one million people had attended the Eucharistic Congress in Dublin, proving, in his opinion, that the city was capable of hosting a massive event like the Olympics.

Speaking in his capacity as President of the NACA in a review of the overall state of athletics in Ireland, O'Duffy complained that Dublin was the only capital city in the world without its own athletics stadium. He also said, 'An athletic stadium in our capital city, which will be the home of our Irish athletes is a national necessity ... Were it not for the kindness of the Gaelic Athletic Association, and other sporting organisations who oblige us with the use of their grounds ... we could not run a sports meeting in Ireland.'

O'Duffy's plan involved the building of a national athletics stadium on the Fifteen-acres in Phoenix Park and he proposed that the project be funded by the government through the use of one or more sweepstakes.

He proposed to build a stadium encompassing five or six acres in the park, describing it as an ideal situation for an Olympic stadium where Ireland's athletes could train under proper conditions 'and where we can stage the athletic section of the Olympic and European Games.' O'Duffy claimed that if the stadium was given the go-ahead by the government, there was no doubt in his mind that Ireland would get an early opportunity to host the European Games even if it failed to secure the Olympic Games for Ireland.

O'Duffy was obviously flying solo on the issue as his plan was not discussed at the NACA's national conference in mid-February that year and he was removed from his post as Garda Commissioner shortly afterwards.

O'Duffy's grand scheme came to nought, and judging by the astronomical amounts of money it costs to host the games these days it's going to be a long time before we see the Olympic flag hoisted over the Fifteen-acres.

Larry

'De Night before Larry was Stretched' was one of at least six versions of a popular Dublin street ballad that was doing the rounds in the late 1780s. All of the songs tell the tale of a condemned prisoner's last night on earth in his cell in Newgate Gaol or Kilmainham and all of them were written in the popular jail slang of the day.

The songs – although written in a highly dramatised fashion – are valuable in that they shine a light on the Dublin criminal classes who lived their lives in the shadow of the scaffold and the 'anatomy men', and they give some insight into the condemned man's last hours before execution.

One version of the ballad, written in 1788, is thought to have been penned in commemoration of the botched execution of an infamous Dublin criminal, Frederick Lambert, on 30 October 1788.

Lambert's life of crime began some five years earlier, when he was convicted in July 1783 for relieving a man of eight shillings and his watch and hat in Arran Street. Lambert – who was only caught because his victim remembered his distinctive limp – didn't fit the usual profile of your average Dublin criminal as his father had been a member of the legal profession and his brother owned a considerable amount of property in the city.

Despite his connections, Lambert was sentenced to death, but he was later given a conditional pardon on the basis that he would leave Ireland for a period of not less than fourteen years.

Lambert left for an unknown destination soon afterwards, but three years later he returned to Dublin and was promptly thrown back into Newgate. He was held on remand for the next two years and in June 1788 he was granted another pardon, which was conditional on him agreeing to be transported not only out of Ireland but also out of Europe for the rest of his life.

Lambert readily agreed to the deal, but while awaiting transportation in Newgate he shared a cell with a violent inmate named Francis Bathhurst who was serving a three-year sentence for throwing a three-year-old boy from a third-storey window. *Walker's Hibernian Magazine* for August 1788 reported on a violent struggle that had taken place in Newgate prison between 'the celebrated Frederic Lambert' and fellow inmate Francis Bathhurst Lambert had apparently tried to engage Bathhurst in a fight, which he refused because of Lambert's disability.

Lambert then slashed Bathurst with a razor and was about to finish him off when he was overpowered by three other prisoners. Bathhurst's wound was treated by the prison surgeon Lake, but it appeared initially that he would die.

However, Bathurst survived and in late October 1788, Lambert was charged with assault under the Chalking Act which allowed convicted criminals to be executed and dissected within two days of sentencing.

Lambert was duly found guilty of maiming Bathurst and the death sentence was carried out on 30 October 1788 on the gallows in front of Newgate prison. However, the execution – which was carried out in front of a huge crowd – didn't go smoothly because the hangman had used the wrong thickness of rope and Lambert was seen to struggle against the rope for several minutes before dying. As the ballad said:

> When he came to de nubbing chit
> He was tucked up so nate and so pretty
> The rumbler shoved off from his feet
> And he died wid his face to the city
> He kicked too but that was all pride
> For soon you may know t'was all over
> And when dat de noose was untied
> At home why we waked him in clover
> And sent him to take a ground sweat ...

Paddy Flemming

The famous old Irish ballad 'Whiskey in the Jar' has been doing the rounds for many years now and the best-known rendition of the song is the one recorded by Dublin band Thin Lizzy in the early 1970s. 'Whiskey in the Jar' has also been covered by a wide range of Irish traditional musicians as well as by bands such as Metallica and The Grateful Dead; and I'm reliably informed that there's at least one rap version of the ballad in existence.

The ballad, in its various forms of 'McCollister' and 'The Irish Robber' has the common theme of highway robbery, betrayal by a faithless woman and eventual execution of the hero. It has been around for well over 200 years and has its origins in a song written to commemorate the life and times of Athlone-born highwayman Patrick Flemming, who ended his days on a Dublin gallows on 24 April 1650.

Flemming's exploits were first mentioned in a line of a ballad entitled 'the Downfall of the Whigs', penned sometime around 1684, and the 'The Ballad of Patrick Flemming' appeared circa 1810, 160 years after his death.

Patrick Flemming, the eldest son in a family of nine children, was born in poor circumstances in Athlone during the early years of the seventeenth century. At the age of thirteen he obtained the position of footboy to the countess of Kildare. However, young Patrick didn't like taking orders from his 'betters' and he was soon shown the door.

Soon afterwards he managed to secure a domestic situation at the home of Lord Antrim but that job didn't last much longer than the first. According to Flemming's biographer, Patrick had a falling out with Lord Antrim's Roman Catholic chaplain and he managed to ridicule the priest in front of the entire household. Flemming was once again given his marching orders but before he left he robbed his employer of silver plate and money to the value of £200.

Flemming lay low for a while after this incident and then made his way to Dublin where he soon earned notoriety as one of the city's most prolific burglars. After a period of about six years, Flemming was forced to flee Dublin because every watchman in the city was on his case. He fled to the midlands where he became a highwayman and he often ventured out from his stronghold in the Bog of Allen to rob passing coaches and other unsuspecting travellers.

Flemming quickly graduated from robbery to murder and he was said to have treated his victims with an 'abundance of barbarity'. He once kidnapped the four-year-old son of Lady Baltimore telling her that he would cut the child's throat and make a pie of him if she didn't pay a ransom within twenty-four hours.

When things got too hot for him in the midlands, Flemming fled to the Munster region to continue his life of crime. He was eventually caught and imprisoned in Cork City but he escaped by climbing up a chimney.

During the years that followed the increasingly desperate Flemming and his gang murdered at least five men, two women and a fourteen-year-old boy and mutilated and tortured many others including Sir Donagh O'Brien who had his ears, nose and lips cut off during a robbery.

Patrick Flemming was eventually captured while drinking at a tavern near Maynooth and taken to Dublin where he was hanged in chains along with fourteen other criminals on 24 April 1650.

First Lord Mayor

The title of mayor of Dublin stretches back nearly eight hundred years to 1229 when Henry III conferred on the citizens of Dublin the right to elect annually from themselves a loyal discreet and proper mayor'. Richard Muton was elected as first mayor of Dublin but the first man to hold the title of lord mayor was Sir Daniel Bellingham – a Dublin gold and silversmith – who held the office in 1665.

Bellingham, who was born circa 1622, became a freeman of the city in 1644 and sheriff of Dublin eleven years later. He became a 'sir' in 1662 and also held the post of vice-treasurer of Ireland from 1663 to 1666.

Prior to holding municipal office in the city, Bellingham was the chief supplier of silver ceremonial objects to the City Assembly and assembly records show that in 1652 'at the request of the Mayor and Sheriffs, he had made six silver maces for the officers following the city sword ...' Bellingham was paid sixty-six pounds sterling and he was given some old city maces and other silver items in part payment for his labours.

However, four years later, Bellingham still hadn't been paid in full for his efforts and in 1656 he petitioned the assembly to pay him the outstanding balance of fifty-seven pounds and three shillings – it was agreed to pay him his money out of fines due to the city. Despite being owed such a large sum, Bellingham still agreed at the same meeting to supply the Assembly with a large silver basket to be put on display with the City Sword.

Bellingham's gold and silver business did very well out of his connection with the city fathers and in 1662, when they decided to present the duke of Ormonde with the freedom of the city and a gold cup and gold box, he was given the lucrative contract of £350 for manufacturing these items.

When Bellingham became lord mayor in 1665 he made himself a great silver mace that was to be carried in civic processions alongside the City Sword. The Great Mace presently in use by Dublin City Council was made by another goldsmith and lord mayor of Dublin, Thomas Bolton, in 1717. This mace is believed to retain some parts of Bellingham's original mace.

When his tenure as lord mayor was over in 1667, Bellingham left the mace to the city and was paid sixty pounds sterling for his trouble.

Gilbert, in his *History of the City of Dublin*, says that Bellingham 'held his mayoralty ... in a large elegant structure, erected by himself across the ancient entrance to Cow Lane at the corner of Fishamble Street and Castle Street'. Gilbert records that in later years, the lord mayor's house was occupied in the mid-eighteenth century by 'an eccentric tobacconist, Thomas Bond and afterwards by another tobacconist named Molony'.

Bellingham was re-elected lord mayor in 1666 but he turned down the offer on the grounds that it would conflict with his duties as deputy receiver of the Exchequer.

Bellingham was a wealthy man at the time of his death in 1671 and he owned a considerable amount of property on the north side of Dublin. In his will he bequeathed some of these lands at Finglas to set up a fund to help prisoners incarcerated in the city's debtors' prisons and the Four Courts Marshalsea Prison.

City Bellman

During medieval times in Dublin the office of city bellman was a much sought-after position. In 1578, the corporation of Dublin selected Dubliner Barnaby Rathe to be the holder of this exalted position, which was similar to that of the English 'town crier'.

The corporation decided that it should get its money's worth from Barnaby and he was also given the titles of 'master of the beggars' and 'over-seer of the swine'.

Barnaby's pig-catching skills must not have been up to much as the City Assembly found it necessary to amend his contract just a few months later. The wandering pig problem was much worse than when Barnaby had started and it was decreed that he would continue to get four pence from every household providing that 'he do his duty in killing such swine as he shall find in the streets, and ridding the city of vagabonds and beggars … it is further agreed that the constables of every warde shall be aiding and helping the said Barnaby for the executing thereof'.

Despite the efforts of the city fathers to help Barnaby, he found the additional role as 'master of the beggars' too much for him and two years later he petitioned the assembly for a place in St John's poorhouse 'without the Newgate' and asked to be relieved of his post as 'beadle of the beggars'. This situation arose because many citizens, who were supposed to pay the four-penny levy for Barnaby's services, refused to do so and the assembly showed no inclination to collect the money by force. The assembly subsequently refused Barnaby's request to give up his post as 'master of the beggars' but did agree to grant him lodgings in the poorhouse.

In June 1581 Barnaby again complained to the assembly that he wasn't being paid for rounding up beggars and again asked to be relieved from his post. His request was again turned down but the assembly did pass extra laws 'to compel the constables of the several wards to levy the said stipend out of several houses of their wards, and in default of payment, the alderman of the ward to commit the partie that doth refuse'.

The measure obviously didn't work as two years later we find that Barnaby 'who hath the greatest part of his wages yet due to him', was back before the assembly again looking for his money. The assembly eventually agreed to pay Barnaby a fixed yearly rate of twenty-six shillings and eight pence for his labours.

His fortunes obviously went from bad to worse after that because eight years later Barnaby, who had lost his job as 'beadle of the beggars' to one John Balloure but retained the post of city bellman, was nearly destitute. He was still in residence at St John's poorhouse in December 1589 and he was in debt to the assembly to the tune of twenty-three shillings sterling.

Although Barnaby spent his last years in the poorhouse, he seems to have been allowed to retain his job as city bellman and he appears to have died in office five years later. The last mention of Barnaby came in 1594 when assembly records stated that: 'John Scally, bellman, shall have the bellman's office, with all prerequisites thereunto belonging, in as large and beneficial manner as Barnaby Rathe, late bellman of this city hath enjoyed ...'

Saint Valentine

Every year on St Valentine's Day, romantic types descend on Dublin's Whitefriar Street Church to visit the shrine of the 'saint of love', but in recent years there has been some controversy as to the real whereabouts of the saint's remains.

The *Catholic Encyclopaedia* lists three different Valentines who were all martyred on 14 February. The first of these was a Roman priest who was martyred in either AD 269 or 270 and the second one was killed while serving as bishop of Terni near Rome. Information in relation to the third Valentine is thin on the ground and the *Catholic Encyclopaedia* only mentions that 'he suffered in Africa with a number of his companions'.

Therefore we don't actually know which Saint Valentine is actually being commemorated on 14 February, but the smart money seems to be on the Roman who was killed during the reign of Claudius the Goth. This Valentine apparently refused to carry out an edict issued by the emperor that forbade all marriages and engagements in Rome because of his belief that married men made poor soldiers. Valentine continued to marry young couples and he was clubbed to death and beheaded for his trouble.

The feast day itself is believed to be a Christian imposition on the pagan Roman festival of Lupercalia, which began on the Ides of February. This was a fertility festival that traditionally began with a visit by the Luperci high priests to the cave where the founders of Rome – Romulus and Remus – were looked after by a she-wolf.

Following the sacrifice of a goat and a dog at the cave, the goat's skin was cut into strips and dipped in blood. The strips were then distributed to young men who would run through the streets of Rome slapping women with them. Far from objecting to the practice, Roman women considered themselves lucky to be slapped with strips of bloody goatskin, as they believed it would make them more fertile. Tradition also has it that the feast of Lupercalia was the time when young Roman men and women chose their partners.

Although the Carmelite church in Dublin's Whitefriar Street claims to hold the remains of Saint Valentine, some other churches also make the same claim. These include the church of Praxedes in Rome and, more recently, St Francis' Church in Glasgow.

While it's quite possible that all the claimants possess a small piece of the saint's remains, the Whitefriar Street case is authenticated by a covering letter from the Vatican, which arrived in Dublin with Saint Valentine's remains in 1836.

One year earlier, a Whitefriar Street priest, Father John Spratt, who was a close friend of Daniel O'Connell, had been preaching in Rome. Father Spratt was renowned in Dublin for his powers of oratory and his work in the poorer areas of the city. While on tour in Rome, he had an audience with Pope Gregory XVI, who honoured him with a gift of the body of Saint Valentine. The saint's remains arrived in Dublin on 10 November 1836 and were taken with great pomp and ceremony to Whitefriar Street Church, where they remain to this day.

Today, the wooden casket holding the saint's remains is on public display at the shrine to Saint Valentine at Whitefriar Street Church and it has become a place of pilgrimage for lovers from all over the world.

Duke of Richmond

Charles Lennox, the duke of Richmond, came to Ireland in 1807 to assume the role of lord lieutenant. Within a short space of time, however, he was better known as the 'duke of Poitín'.

The duke – after whom the Richmond Penitentiary and Richmond Lunatic Asylum were later named – arrived here to take up residence at Dublin Castle and his tenure was marked by feasting and drinking on a grand scale.

Lennox was more intent on the pursuit of pleasure than attending to affairs of state during his reign in Ireland, and it was said that he would think nothing of knocking back four bottles of claret with his dinner.

He took an active role in Dublin's social life and he would often be seen at events such as the Donnybrook Fair and the annual pattern at St John's Well near Kilmainham, where he presided over sumptuous feasts laid on for his cronies and hangers-on.

The duke also liked his sport and he was a regular visitor to cock-fighting bouts in Clarendon Street and he was also fond of boxing and cricket. However, his favourite pastime was the game of rackets – an early form of tennis – which he played regularly at the rackets hall in John's Lane.

Richmond liked to amuse himself by bringing over some of England's top players for matches and one of these was Lord Sydney Osborne, who prided himself on his skill with a racket. On one visit to Dublin he challenged 'any man in the world' to play him for a wager of a thousand guineas.

Along with his other vices, the duke of Richmond was also an inveterate gambler and he promised Osborne that he would find a worthy opponent for him. The man that the duke had in mind was a Dublin tailor named Flood, who also happened to be a highwayman and pickpocket in his spare time. Flood was also handy with a racket and the duke had seen him play on a number of occasions at the John's Lane court.

The morning after striking the bet with Osborne, Richmond hurried off to the court to find Flood but was dismayed to discover that the tailor was lying in a cell in Newgate Prison, where he was due to be hanged for highway robbery on the following Saturday.

The duke quickly organised a pardon for the tailor and Flood was duly freed. Richmond soon made Flood aware of the real reason he had been released and the grateful tailor promised that he would win his bet for him.

The day of the match duly arrived and Osborne, who didn't know a thing about Richmond's little scheme, started the game brimming with confidence. He began the match well, but Flood slowly wore him down and gradually began to get on top of Osborne. Frustrated by the prospect of being beaten by a lowly tailor, Osborne soon lost his temper and ultimately the match and his wager with the duke of Richmond.

The duke gave Flood fifty pounds for winning the match and advised him to leave the country – but he decided to stay in Dublin and try to resurrect his career as a tailor. However, he was unable to shake off the stigma of his criminal past and no one would employ him. Flood eventually changed his name to Waters and moved to London, where he found employment as a scorekeeper at the Tottenham Court Road rackets court.

The duke of Richmond left Dublin in 1813 and he died from rabies in 1819 after being bitten by his pet fox.

Father Fay

The name of eighteenth-century Dublin priest Father Patrick Fay is not one that you're likely to find mentioned in the *Catholic Encyclopaedia* and it's a safe bet that he'll never get on a short-list for canonisation.

'Father' Fay was originally a Roman Catholic priest in Dublin during the 1780s but this colourful clergyman was better known in the city for his extra-curricular activities such as common assault, forgery and wrestling. Fay was also a successful property speculator and he also ran a lucrative practice as a 'couple-beggar'.

A couple-beggar can be best described as an unscrupulous priest who would marry anyone, regardless of age or station, and the only criterion was that they paid the priest's exorbitant marriage fee. Fay was known to charge couples a guinea for the privilege and was said to marry up to six couples a day.

Fay publicly renounced his faith and joined the Church of Ireland and bought himself the chaplaincy of the Royal Hospital at Kilmainham. He didn't last too long in this position, however, as he was dismissed for inappropriate behaviour.

It was after his dismissal from his post at Kilmainham that Fay first hit on the idea of becoming a couple-beggar and he soon developed a thriving practice from one of his many Dublin homes.

Following several years of litigation in the Dublin courts, the archbishop of Dublin managed to get all of these marriages annulled. However, this didn't bother Father Fay in the slightest and he carried on regardless.

Father Fay was also known to be quick with his fists and was adept at wrestling. In 1786 Fay was brought before a Dublin court on 27 October where he was indicted on a charge of 'assaulting and cutting in a most dangerous manner' one Bridget Duffy at Drumcondra in August of that year. He was initially sentenced to six months in Newgate but managed to stay out of jail by paying off his victim.

In April of the following year the *Freeman's Journal* reported on a wrestling match between Fay and a sedan-chair carrier which was held in a field near Phibsborough. In the fight, which was witnessed by a large crowd Fay eventually defeated the 'chairman', winning a gallon of whiskey for his troubles.

In September 1788, Patrick Fay, who was by that time being described as a widower and father of five children, was accused and found guilty of forgery and sentenced to be hanged at Newgate prison on 8 November of that year. The Reverend Fay was indicted on four counts of forgery and with intent to defraud two Harristown farmers, Patrick Fulham and his brother John, and the high sheriff of County Meath.

At the time that the sentence was passed, Fay was given no chance of a reprieve and *Walkers Hibernian Magazine* of September in 1788 reported: 'His being known to be a man of affluence, and under no pressure of necessity, to cause his having recourse to such a criminal expedient, weighs chiefly against him as he is supposed to be the proprietor of at least a dozen houses in Dublin.'

Despite the paper's pessimism, Fay did manage to have his sentence commuted to transportation and on 13 June 1789 he was taken from Kilmainham prison and put on board the *Duke of Leinster* which was bound for Nova Scotia.

However, Fay never reached his destination and it subsequently emerged that he had paid the ship's captain to allow him to escape on board a fishing vessel while they were still close to the Irish coast. He subsequently settled in the French city of Bordeaux where newspaper reports say he became a successful cheesemonger.

Constable Sheahan

At three o'clock in the afternoon on Saturday 6 May 1905, a fitter working on the Dublin main drainage scheme, John Fleming, climbed down into a sewer at the junction of Burgh Quay and Hawkins Street in order to fix a broken pipe.

He had hardly reached the bottom of the ladder when noxious fumes rising from the sewer overcame him. Two of his workmates who tried to go to his assistance were also struck down by the deadly gases.

A young newspaper boy named Christopher Nolan, who witnessed the incident, ran to get help. The first person he came across was twenty-eight-year-old DMP constable Patrick Sheahan, who was on duty at the nearby O'Connell Bridge.

Sheahan, described as being of 'Herculean proportions', had been in tight situations before. Three years earlier he had rescued an elderly couple from a falling tenement in Townsend Street and he once single-handedly recaptured an escaped bull in Grafton Street.

Sheahan rushed to the scene of the accident and climbed down into the manhole, where he managed to get Fleming and his workmate John Coleman back to the surface. However, Fleming, a resident of Gordon Street in Ringsend and father of nine children, never regained consciousness and died soon after arriving at Mercer's Hospital. Sheahan himself fell victim to the poisonous vapours shortly afterwards and perished at the bottom of the sewer.

A large number of spectators had gathered at the scene and the *Dublin Evening Mail* described the crowd as 'hooligans of the worst possible type, utterly indifferent to all considerations save their own contemptible amusement, and to them anything in the shape of interference with the police was enjoyable'.

However, the *Mail* journalist seems to have gotten his story badly wrong on this occasion as it subsequently emerged that many of these so-called 'hooligans' had recklessly risked their own lives in an attempt to rescue the men trapped in the drain.

Time and time again, firemen and members of the public descended into the sewer in a vain attempt to rescue Sheahan, but many were overcome by the gases and had to be rescued themselves. Apart from the two dead men, nine rescuers were eventually hauled from the sewer in an unconscious state.

The heroism demonstrated by Sheahan and the other rescuers had a deep impact on the city, and thousands of Dubliners came out to pay their respects when Sheahan's remains were taken from Mercer's Hospital to lie overnight at Mount Argus before being transported to his native Limerick for burial.

At an inquest into the tragedy a few days later, the Dublin City coroner was fulsome in his praise of the crowd and he particularly singled out Irishtown hackney-cab driver Kieran Fitzpatrick and fireman Martin Lambert for their heroism. Fitzpatrick and Lambert were awarded gallantry medals later on for their actions on that day. In all, thirty members of the public and two firemen were presented with medals for their heroism.

The lord mayor of Dublin made a public appeal for funds to build a suitable memorial on the spot to Constable Sheahan and the others who took part in the rescue; and the monument designed by a Mr P. O'Neill, which now commemorates their deeds on the corner of Burgh Quay and Hawkins Street, was erected in 1906 by the Mansion House Committee.

Frank De Groot

Official records show that the opening of the famous Sydney Harbour Bridge took place on 19 March 1932 when the Premier of New South Wales, J.T. Lang, performed the ribbon-cutting ceremony.

Unofficially however – and much to the embarrassment of the Australian authorities – the bridge received an unscheduled opening moments earlier when Dublin fascist, Captain Frank De Groot, dressed in an Australian army uniform and mounted on a horse, charged forward and slashed the ribbon with his sword declaring the bridge open 'in the name of the decent and respectable people of New South Wales'.

Captain De Groot had managed to avoid detection by riding on to the bridge along with the official Governors' mounted escort and he wasn't apprehended until after he had declared the bridge officially open.

De Groot was dragged from his horse after the incident,

arrested and charged with insanity, insulting behaviour and threatening a police inspector. He was examined by a 'mental specialist' who declared that he could find nothing wrong with the captain.

Frank De Groot was born at Lakesfield, Strand Road in Merrion in 1890 and was a member of a well-known Dublin Huguenot family. He was educated at Blackrock College and emigrated to Australia soon after finishing his studies and became an antiques and fine arts dealer.

He returned to Dublin soon after the outbreak of the First World War where he enlisted as an officer in the British Army. He served with the 15th Hussars in France during the war and afterwards returned to Australia. There he resumed his former occupation as an art dealer and also became a commander in the fascist and anti-communist New Guard movement in New South Wales.

Following the bridge incident, one English newspaper alleged that De Groot had served with the Black and Tans in Ireland during the War of Independence, but his family strenuously denied this.

De Groot appeared before Sydney's Lunacy Court on a charge of being insane but the case was dismissed. However, the Dubliner was rearrested and charged with malicious damage to the ribbon, which was valued at two pounds.

De Groot was brought before the police court at Liverpool Street in Sydney on 1 April 1932 and his trial attracted a crowd of over 3,000, which included members of the New Guard and a great number of communists. Two hundred policemen marshalled the crowd and ten arrests were made.

De Groot was remanded on the ribbon-slashing charge but was given bail when the commander-in-chief of the New Guard put up bail for his release. The Australian public greeted the incident with some hilarity and a 'De Groot shilling fund' was established in his honour. Within two days, the fund had reached 2,500 shillings.

The fund was established by a Sydney solicitor who compared De Groot's actions to the Boston Tea Party, which triggered the American War of Independence.

De Groot was later charged with assaulting the police and his trial began on 4 April. De Groot said that he had decided to cut the ribbon himself because, in his opinion, 'he was much better suited to open the bridge than Mr Lang because of his [De Groot's] superior war service'.

De Groot was convicted on the insulting behaviour charge and was fined the maximum fine of five pounds. He later sued the police and the chief secretary of New South Wales for £5,000 in damages and the claim was eventually settled out of court.

Frank De Groot eventually returned to Ireland and he died here in 1969.

Howth Disaster

On 15 February 1853, the *Queen Victoria* steamship belonging to the City of Dublin Steam-packet Company, ran aground near the Bailey Lighthouse in Howth, resulting in the sinking of the ship and the loss of seventy passengers and crew. The

Queen Victoria struck rocks near the Bailey during a blizzard and went down about fifteen minutes later.

The *Queen Victoria* had set out on its short voyage from Liverpool to Dublin on the afternoon of Monday 14 February with a mixed cargo and approximately 120 people on board under the command of Captain Church, a skipper of many years experience.

All went well until the ship ran into a heavy snowstorm in the Irish Sea. Despite the blizzard, however, the *Queen Victoria* managed to make steady progress and by 2 a.m. it had passed the Kish Lighthouse. Soon the Bailey Lighthouse came into view momentarily but at that stage the snow became so dense that it was completely blocked from view.

With visibility down to zero, the ship's lookout didn't see the rugged cliffs of Howth until they were fifty yards away and, despite a desperate attempt to stop the ship, it smashed headlong onto the jagged rocks at a spot called the Broken Hatchets.

Captain Church gave orders to reverse the ship's engines and he succeeded in steering the steamer away from the rocks into deeper water, but the ship had been badly holed beneath the waterline and began to sink rapidly.

Many of the ship's passengers, who had been asleep below deck, rushed towards the ship's lifeboats. One lifeboat wasn't secured properly and fell straight into the freezing waters, killing all of its occupants instantly.

Another lifeboat with seventeen people aboard was successfully launched, but it was found to be leaking rapidly until a young boy, showing great presence of mind, thrust his hand into the plughole and plugged the leak.

Despite the captain's efforts to calm them, many men, women and children left on board the stricken ship panicked and leapt into the sea and were drowned instantly. The *Queen Victoria* went down shortly afterwards and Captain Church, in true seafaring tradition, went down with his craft.

However, the masts of the ship were still visible above the waterline and at least a dozen survivors clung desperately to the foremast and mainmast. The lifeboat manned by the boy with his hand in the plughole and other crew members bravely returned to the ship and rescued five survivors off the topmast and were about to attempt the rescue of the others when the steamer *Roscommon* arrived on the scene and took off the remaining survivors.

In all, fifty-eight persons managed to survive the disaster, including twenty members of the crew. Those rescued by the *Roscommon* were safely landed the next day at Kingstown (Dun Laoghaire) while those rescued by the heroic lifeboat men were landed at Howth. In addition to these were ten or twelve of the passengers and crew who had managed to jump onto the rocks when the ship first struck and were helped to safety by the keeper of the Bailey Lighthouse.

An inquiry into the disaster later concluded that the *Victoria* was lost through the negligence of Captain Church 'in not sounding, stopping the engines, or taking proper precautions when the snow-shower came on' and the conduct of the first mate was also sited as a major cause of the disaster. The head of the inquiry, Captain W.H. Walker, also observed that the accident might have been avoided if the Bailey Lighthouse had been properly manned and fitted with a fog-bell. Captain Walker also commended the young seaman Patrick D'Arcy for his quick thinking in plugging the hole in the lifeboat with his hand.

SELECT BIBLIOGRAPHY

Andrews, C.S., *Dublin Made Me* (Mercier Press, Cork, 1979)

Anon., *The Life and Times of G.R. Fitzgerald* (Dublin, 1787)

Ball, F.E., *A History of the County Dublin* (Alexander Thom, Dublin, 1906)

Barrington, J., *Personal Sketches of his Own Times* (London, 1830–2)

Bennett, D., *Encyclopaedia of Dublin* (Gill & Macmillan, Dublin, 2005)

Boylan, H., *A Dictionary of Irish Biography* (Gill & Macmillan, Dublin, 1978)

Burton, N.J., *Letters from Harold's Cross 1850* (Carrig Books, Dublin, 1979)

Cameron, C.H., *History of the Royal College of Surgeons* (Dublin, 1910)

Chart, D.A., *Dublin* (J.M. Dent, London, 1907)

Clarke, HB., (ed.), *Medieval Dublin: The Making of a Metropolis* (Dublin, 1990)

Clarke, H.B. (ed.), *Medieval Dublin: The Living City* (Dublin, 1990)

Coates T. (ed.), *The Irish Uprising 1914-21* (The Stationery Office Ltd., Norwich, 2000)

Collins, J., *Life in Old Dublin*, (James Duffy & Co., Dublin, 1913)

Cosgrave, D., *North Dublin City and Environs* (Four Courts Press, Dublin, 1909)

Cowell, J., *Where they lived in Dublin* (O'Brien Press, Dublin, 1980)

Craig, M., *Dublin 1660–1860* (Allen Figgis, Dublin, 1969)

Crawford, J., *Within the Walls: The Story of St Audoen's Church, Corn-market, Dublin* (Select Vestry of the St Patrick's Cathedral Group of Parishes, Dublin, 1986)

D'Alton, J., *The History of the County Dublin* (Hodges and Smith, Dublin, 1838)

De Courcy, J.W., *The Liffey in Dublin* (Gill & Macmillan, Dublin, 1996)

Dickson, D., (ed.), *The Gorgeous Mask: Dublin 1700–1850* (Trinity History Workshop, Dublin, 1987)

Dixon, D. *Arctic Ireland - the extraordinary story of the Great Frost and forgotten famine of 1740–41* (White Row Press Ltd., Belfast, 1997)

Dudley, R., *The Irish Lottery 1780–1801* (Four Courts Press, Dublin, 2005)

Fagan, Terry, *Monto: Madams Murder and Black Coddle*, (North Inner City Folklore Group, Dublin 2000)

Fitzpatrick, W.J., *Memoirs of Richard Whately* (London, 1864)

Fitzpatrick, W.J., *The Sham Squire, and the Informers of 1798* (London, 1866)

Fleetwood, J., *The Irish Body Snatchers: A History of Body Snatching in Ireland* (Tomar Publishing Ltd., Dublin, 1988)

Flint, J., *The Dublin Police and the Police System* (Dublin, 1847)

Gilbert, Sir J.T., *A History of the City of Dublin*, (3 vols, Vol.1, Dublin, James McGlashan, 1854; Vols 2 & 3, Dublin: McGlashan and Gill, 1859)

Gilbert, Sir J.T. (ed.) and Gilbert, Lady, *Calendar of Ancient Records of Dublin* (19 Volumes, Joseph Dollard, Dublin, 1889–1944)

Gilligan, H.A., *History of the Port of Dublin* (Dublin, 1988)

Haliday, C., *The Scandinavian Kingdom of Dublin* (Alexander Thom, Dublin 1881)

Harris, W., *History of the Antiquities of the City of Dublin* (L. Flynn, Dublin, 1766)

Harrison, W., *Memorable Dublin Houses* (Dublin, 1890)

Henry, B., *Dublin Hanged – Crime, law enforcement and punishment in late eighteenth-century Dublin* (Irish Academic Press, Dublin, 1994)

Herlihy, J., *The Dublin Metropolitan Police, A Short History and Genealogical Guide* (Fourt Courts Press, Dublin, 2001)

Hoare, Sir Richard, *Journal of a tour in Ireland, A.D. 1806* (London, 1807)

Hogan, R., *Dion Boucicault* (Twayne, New York, 1969)

Igoe, V., *Dublin Burial Grounds and Graveyards* (Wolfhound Press, Dublin, 2001)

Joyce, Weston St. John, *The Neighbourhood of Dublin* (Dublin, 1921)

Kelly, F., *A History of Kilmainham Gaol* (Mercier Press, Cork, 1988)

Kelly, J., *Gallows Speeches from Eighteenth-Century Ireland* (Four Courts Press, Dublin, 2001)

Kelly, M., *The Great Dying – The Black Death in Dublin* (Tempus Publishing Ltd., Gloucestershire, 2003)

Knapp and Baldwin (eds.), *Newgate Calendar* (3 vols., London, 1824)

Lambert, R.S., *The Prince of Pickpockets: A Study of George Barrington Who Left His Country for His Country's Good* (Faber & Faber, London, 1930)

Langtry, J. and Carter N. (editors), *Mount Jerome – A Victorian Cemetery* (Mount Jerome Historical Project, Dublin, 1997)

Lee, G.A., *Leper Hospitals in Medieval Ireland* (Four Courts Press, Dublin, 1996)

Leeson, M., (ed. Lyons, M.), *Memoirs of Mrs Margaret Leeson* (Lilliput Press (reprint), Dublin, 1995)

Lewis, S., *A Topographical Dictionary of Ireland*, (Lewis & Co., London, 1837)

Little, G.A., *Malachi Horan Remembers* (M.H. Gill and Son, Dublin, 1944)

Lyons, J.B., *The Quality of Mercer's: The Story of Mercer's Hospital 1734–1991* (Glendale Publishing Ltd., Dublin, 1991)

McCall, P.J., *In the Shadow of St. Patrick's* (Dublin, 1894)

McCready, C.T., *Dublin Street Names, Dated and Explained* (Hodges Figgis, Dublin, 1892)

McGregor, J., *New picture of Dublin* (Dublin, 1828)

Madden, R.R., *The United Irishmen, their lives and times* (Mullany, Dublin, 1860)

Malcolm, E., *Swift's Hospital* (Gill & Macmillan, Dublin, 1989)

Maxwell, C., *Dublin under the Georges* (George Harrap, London, 1946)

Maxwell, C., *The Stranger in Ireland* (Jonathan Cape, Dublin, 1954)

Porter F.T., *Twenty years' recollections of an Irish police magistrate* (Hodges, Foster and Figgis, Dublin, 1880)

O'Keefe, J., *Recollections* (London, 1826)

Snoddy, T., *Dictionary of Irish Artists 20th Century* (Wolfhound Press, Dublin, 1996)

Walsh, J.E., *Sketches of Ireland Sixty Years Ago* (London, 1847)

Warburton, J., Whitelaw, J., Walsh, R., *History of the city of Dublin*, (London, 1818)

Webb, J.J, *The Guilds of Dublin* (Benn, Dublin, 1929)

Wright, G.N. *An historical guide to ancient and modern Dublin* (London, 1821)

Wright, GN., *Life and campaigns of Arthur, duke of Wellington K.G.* (London, 1841)

Magazines, Newspapers, Periodicals, Journals etc.:

Dublin Chronicle

Dublin Courant

Dublin Evening Mail

Dublin Evening Post

Dublin Historical Record

Dublin Penny Journal

Dublin Newsletter

Dublin University Magazine

Evening Herald

Faulkner's Dublin Journal

Freeman's Journal

Garda Review

Gentleman's Magazine

Hibernian Journal

Irish Builder & Engineer

Irish Ecclesiastical Record

Irish Independent

Irish Press

Irish Times

Irish Worker

Journal of the Royal Society of Antiquaries of Ireland

Magee's Weekly Packet

Pue's Occurrences

Saunders' Newsletter

Times (London)

Walker's Hibernian Magazine

SCALES

DUBLIN